P9-CRK-262

Striving Toward Virtue

A Contemporary Guide for
Jewish Ethical Behavior

Striving Toward Virtue

A Contemporary Guide for Jewish Ethical Behavior

by

Rabbi Kerry M. Olitzky

and

Rabbi Rachel T. Sabath

KTAV Publishing House, Inc.
Hoboken, New Jersey

Library of Congress Cataloging-in-Publication Data

Olitzky, Kerry M.
    Striving toward virtue : a contemporary guide for Jewish ethical behavior / by
Kerry M. Olitzky and Rachel T. Sabath.
      p.   cm.
    At head of title: Madreigot ha-middot.
    ISBN 0-88125-534-3
    1. Ethics, Jewish. 2. Conduct of life.   I. Sabath, Rachel T., 1968–   . II. Title.
III: Title: Madreigot ha-middot
BJ1287.055S87   1996
296.3' 85—dc20   96-17734
                                            CIP

Manufactured in the United States of America

For
Rabbi Eugene B. Borowitz,
our teacher and colleague

The reward of reverence is Torah
(Shemot Rabbah 40:1)

Contents

Moving Toward God

Acknowledgments

It is never easy for two people to write a book together. But it is a form of cooperative learning, a *chevruta* of sorts, a current thread in the educational tapestry of modern education. In writing this, our second coauthored project, we have proven that student and teacher can become colleagues, and that colleagues can become friends. While it is also difficult for two people to write with one voice and to speak in the first person, we have tried to speak as one voice, except where the subject does not allow us to do so. This is particularly the case with some of the personal anecdotes and illustrations which are scattered throughout the pages. Instead of trying to identify the coauthor associated with each memory, we hope that the reader will identify with the illustration or anecdote and not worry about its provenance.

Together, our appreciation goes to Bernard Scharfstein of KTAV Publishing House, who invited us to develop this volume; his keen sense of Jewish publishing is reflected in its pages. In his person, Bernard reflects much of what we are trying to teach. We also want to thank Professor Mark Kligman, who reviewed this material and offered us his gentle insights. His friendship is bound within each of our words. By her suggestions, Rabbi Robyn Tsesarsky helped place us on course as the idea for this book began to take shape. To her, our thanks are likewise due.

From Kerry: My thanks go to my parents, Abe and Frances Olitzky, who taught me the value of the concepts treated in this book by embedding them within the Yiddishe home they sought to create in a South that was not always welcoming to them. To my children, Avi and Jesse, who remind me of the importance of these values each day. And to my spouse, my life's partner, Sheryl, who models these values so that I might learn them each day anew.

From Rachel: I am grateful to my parents, Suzanne Wells Sabath and Leon D. Sabath, and to my sisters, Natasha and Joanna, who modeled in different ways many of the virtues discussed in this volume. I am also aware of the enormous influence of many members of two different communities of teachers and colleagues who have challenged me to seek a higher level of ethical Jewish living: Hebrew Union College–Jewish Institute of Religion (members of both the Jerusalem and New York campuses) and the Wexner Graduate Fellowship Program. I am especially grateful to Kerry Olitzky for inviting me to create this book in *chevruta*-style. Similarly, I am particularly appreciative of one my mentors, Rabbi Joseph Edelheit.

I am grateful to Rabbis Andrea C. London, Leon Morris and Yael Ridberg who shared with me their endless friendship, words of Torah and encouraged me without fail to struggle toward seeking to fulfill each of these *middot*. In my own climbing toward a higher level of intellectual and spiritual communion with God, I have relied heavily on the teachings of the early Hasidim. In particular, I have grown in a loving *chevruta* I share with Shaul Magid.

* * *

This book is dedicated to Rabbi Eugene B. Borowitz, who teaches and inspires moral piety through the study and application of *middot* and who continues to offer a *musar* teaching to whoever listens to his Torah. To the extent to which each of us has internalized his teachings, his voice can be heard in this pages. He made this book conceivable by insisting that the Torah we might teach be heard in our day.

Kerry Marc Olitzky
Rachel Tatiana Sabath

While every effort has been made to trace and acknowledge all copyright holders, we would like to apologize for any omissions. We have also tried to trace all sources of our sacred oral and written traditions, including the teachings of Hasidic masters. We were not always successful in doing so. We acknowledge with deep appreciation the following individuals, who have graciously agreed to allow us to reprint some of their words: Rabbi Eugene B. Borowitz; Rabbi Nina Beth Cardin and *Sh'ma*; Rabbi Daniel Freelander and Cantor Jeff Klepper; Joel Grishaver; Dr. Abraham J. Karp; Dr. Reuven Kimelman; Rabbi Zalman Schacter-Shalomi; Rabbi Harold Schulweis; Rabbi Rami Shapiro; Danny Siegel; and Rabbi Chaim Stern. We also wish to acknowledge the following: *Teshuvah: A Guide for the Newly Observant Jew* by Rabbi Adin Steinsaltz. Copyright © 1982 by The Domino Press, Jerusalem. English translation by Michael Swirsky, Copyright © 1987 by The Free Press, a division of Simon & Schuster; excerpt from *God in Search of Man: A Philosophy of Judaism* by Abraham Heschel. Renewed © 1983 by Sylvia Heschel. Farrow, Straus & Giroux, Inc. Reprinted by permission.

A note to the reader: We have chosen to use many Hebrew concept words in this book, because we feel that the Hebrew often expresses certain values and concepts in ways that no other language can. While we affirm that "all translation is interpretation," we have generally translated Hebrew words into English at least the first time they are used. However, you may always refer to the Glossary of Terms and Concepts at the end of the book.

Introduction

Usually we think of Judaism with regard to the ultimate questions, probing ancient sources in order to gain insight on the meaning of life and its daily challenges. We focus our attention on sacred texts because they provide us with a timeless prism through which we are able to peer into our own soul and move it to higher levels of morality, humanity, and holiness. Because Torah captures the divine light which allows us to see ourselves more clearly, regular study helps us to keep our lives in balance, bringing us a sense of stability in a rocky and fragile world.

Such study is best done with another person, a *chevruta*, or "study partner." Yet as we study, we do not look for singular answers or truths. That would rob us of the opportunity, even the necessity, to struggle with the text, to find ourselves in it, to make it our own, to continue asking questions and thereby join with those who came before us in the Jewish textual tradition.

Nevertheless, as human beings we acknowledge the unique nature of the individual and the journey we each must take alone. So we look to the teachers, both past and present, who have guidance to offer us about the moral life: how we ought to behave and what our relationships with other people and with the Supreme Being should be. On their shoulders we stand.

Middot, as Jewish tradition calls the pieces of focused moral guidance for daily living that it offers us, are possibilities in everyday life. We are all ideally capable of doing any of them. But we must build around them and make them meaningful in our daily reality; otherwise they are an evaporating source of moral strength. And the moral fiber of our lives is weakened.

As we consider the *middot* together with the consequences of our actions, we can realign our lives and make sure we are going in the right direction, spiraling upward toward a life in concert with what God demands of us as partners in the continuous creation and restoration of an imperfect but redeemable world.

Following the advice provided in this book, which is permeated with and reflective of Jewish tradition, we hope you will find yourself motivated to spiral upward by developing *middot tovot* (positive moral attributes). Rather than presenting an academic discussion of these moral virtues, we have worked to reframe them as reflections of our own experiences and the experiences of those with whom we have studied, articulating them in a voice which you, the reader, will readily hear and will find relevant in your daily life.

We speak as rabbis and teachers, but most of all we speak as individuals, sharing and working together yet nonetheless separate entities in the cosmos, who perceive ourselves as very much similar to our readers, since we are all human sisters and brothers, and therefore striving upwards in an ascending spiral toward holiness and, we pray, toward God.

The Hebrew title of this work is *Madreigot Ha-Middot* ("The Stairway of Virtues"), implying that the *middot* it presents afford us with the opportunity to advance gradually upward in our journey to meet God and, through the process, find a heightened and deeper moral understanding of ourselves. This is intentionally not a very large book. It is designed simply to inspire you to climb higher than where you currently stand, and to provide you with a spiritual reference point firmly based in the Jewish textual tradition.

This book offers basic insights drawn from Jewish sacred sources and from contemporary writings. Our contribution is informed by the classic *Sefer Ma'alot Ha-Middot* by Yehiel ben Yekutiel ben Benyamin Ha-Rofe of Rome in the late thirteenth century. In his book,

Yehiel ben Yekutiel blended together biblical and rabbinic statements as insights on moral living, categorizing them into twenty-
four virtues and vices.

Once upon a time it would have been enough to offer readers the
book that Yehiel prepared, in which he argued for the various virtues solely based on the force behind them in our tradition. Nowadays, for many reasons, many of us need much more than a reprise
of the words of the tradition on any given subject. Words and ideas
are irrelevant if we do not know how to apply them to our own
lives.

A disappointed student once complained to a teacher, "I have
been through the Talmud several times, and have learned nothing
about my life." Came the teacher's response, "But how many times
has the Talmud been through you?"

While we have included a selection of passages from Yehiel ben
Yekutiel's book in this work, we believe that a new structure is
needed to meet the need of contemporary Jews to study the tradition on their own and to find a way for the tradition to go through
them as individuals. Our book also takes into consideration the
efforts of modern secular educators like William Bennett, who in
his recent best-seller, *The Book of Virtues*, challenged Americans to
revisit some of the ethical principles and values on which this
nation was founded. In his volume, Bennett provided readers with a
myriad of sources for study and reflection.

Likewise, this volume emanates from some of the ideas developed by our teacher and colleague Eugene B. Borowitz. Like him,
we seek to present classic Jewish wisdom to readers who are looking for a contemporary approach to moral virtue which is informed
by classic Jewish sources.

Perhaps our goal in preparing this modest volume is best summarized by these words of midrash:

> How do we find our Parent in Heaven? We find God by doing
> good deeds and studying Torah. How does the Holy One find us?
> God finds us through love, harmony, reverence, companionship,
> truth, peace, humility, modesty, more study, less commerce, service

to the wise, discussions with students, decency, a no that is really no
and a yes that is really yes.

Seder Eliyahu Rabbah 23

The author of this text understood that morality is found in the
committed relationships that we develop with God and with our
fellow human beings. Since each *middah* described in this book
impacts on our relationships with self, others, and God, we have
divided the volume into three sections, focusing respectively on
middot which are best expressed through the classic contextualiza-
tions of God, self, and others, reconfigured and framed as "Turning
Toward Self," "Reaching Toward Others," and "Moving Toward
God."

The idea of constant movement is central to this pedagogy. The
middot are ordered in the way we see the upward spiral of *middot*
moving in the life of an individual; from self, to others, and ultimately toward God. Included in each chapter, under the rubric
"Knowing, Being, Doing," we recommend things one might do,
some of which we try to do in our own lives and have encouraged
others to do in their lives. These activities are designed to simultaneously strengthen ourselves and others and heal our fractured
world. At the end of each chapter, we have added some additional
middot material for further contemplation, culled from a variety of
sources which reflect the diversity of Jewish writing on ethical
issues.

In compiling this volume we have had one goal in mind: to help
you consider your behaviors and the life you choose to lead, to
guide you higher and higher toward the fulfillment of our creation—living fully as you are, *betzelem elohim*, created in the image
of God.

Madreigot Ha-Middot

The Stairway of Virtues

*If you have repented, do not imagine that you are far
below the level of the righteous because of the iniquities and sins you have committed; it is not so. Instead,
you are as beloved and precious to the Creator as you
would have been if you had never sinned at all. Indeed,
your reward is especially great, for even though you
have tasted sin, you have broken away from it and
overcome your evil inclination. Accordingly, the sages
said, "In a place where the repentant stand, the completely righteous may not stand." That is to say, penitents stand on a higher rung than those who have
never sinned, because they had to make a greater effort
to subdue their evil impulses.*

Babylonian Talmud, Berachot 34b

CHAPTER 1

Going Backwards/Making the Turn
Yeridah/Teshuvah

A young prince once left his father's house and ventured out on his own. He wandered for many years, enjoying his independence, tasting fruits unavailable in the palace. In time, as he matured, he realized that he had strayed too far. He wanted to return home, but found that he didn't have enough money for the journey. He sent word to the palace, asking his father, the king, to come and bring him home. The reply: "I will meet you halfway."

adapted from Pesikta Rabbati 44

Turning, turning, turning. That's what significant life changes are about: repeatedly turning, and then facing in another direction, turning toward God. If you really want to rearrange your life, there is only one way to do it: turn inside yourself, and then turn outside. Face in a new direction to gain perspective, then gather the strength to make the journey forward.

The first turn is the hardest. As Rav Avraham Kook, the first Ashkenazi chief rabbi of Israel, once said, the road of repentance is narrow and twisting. It does not follow a straight path; and neither do our lives. There will be some *yeridah*, some downward spiraling. What helps motivate us to get on the path in the first place and strive to move forward is the knowledge that God is prepared to meet us halfway and accompany us the rest of the way home.

In Jewish tradition, this process of change is called *teshuvah*. The word *teshuvah*, often translated as "repentance," "renewal," or "respiritualization," literally means "turning" or "returning," coming back, coming home, directing our lives with a holy purpose. Recognizing God's central presence in our lives is what makes a change *teshuvah* and not just a reorganization of life priorities when the pressures of job and family collide. A student once asked a rabbi, "How will I know when I'm on the right track?" The answer, "Asking the question shows that you're moving in the right direction."

The Jewish calendar encourages us to concentrate on changing (repenting) at certain specific times. During Elul, the month immediately preceding the High Holy Days, we strive to become especially introspective and focus our attention on the hard work of *teshuvah*. This period of penetrating self-scrutiny leads us upwards to its culmination on Yom Kippur, the Day of Atonement and brings us toward Simchat Torah.

In addition, the beginning of every month (Rosh Chodesh) is called a Yom Kippur Katan (a mini–Yom Kippur) because it too is a time when we can review our lives and start again—born anew, as some kabbalists suggest, in the new month.

But the opportunity to do *teshuvah* is not restricted to specific times. It is always available. One of the blessings included in the *Amidah* (*Shemoneh Esreh*), the core prayer of our liturgy, encourages us to do *teshuvah* each day: "Help us, our Creator, to return to Your Torah. Draw us near, our Sovereign, to Your service. Bring us back into Your presence with full repentance. Praised are You, Eternal One, who delights in repentance."

Some say that we must actively seek God at every opportunity and not just in the process of *teshuvah*. If opportunities to "do *teshuvah*" are set aside throughout the year, we have no reason to procrastinate our *teshuvah* work until we can get around to it. However, in anticipation of Yom Kippur (the ultimate day for intense personal growth and spiritual renewal), God comes looking for us. This makes the *teshuvah* work of the High Holy Days more urgent. As Rabbi Samuel ben Nachman once suggested, "The gates of prayer are sometimes open and sometimes closed, but the gates of repentance are always open. Just as the sea is always accessible, so the hand of the Holy Blessed One is always open to receive penitents" (Deuteronomy Rabbah 2:12).

But *teshuvah* is not a goal to be attained; it is not a place we can ever really reach. It is an ongoing process, an attitude toward life, and as Professor Bernard Reisman of Brandeis University is fond of saying, we must "trust the process." We cannot realize the power of *teshuvah* to transform our lives until we commit ourselves to it. If we do, it can change our whole perspective. By means of *teshuvah*, every day and in every way, we can work to improve ourselves, undaunted by the awareness that we will never really get there and will sometimes fall down, fall backwards.

After a while, as we engage in the process of *teshuvah*-change, we come to realize that its culmination is deliberately just beyond our reach, prodding us to reach further beyond ourselves and deeper within ourselves. Remarkably, as we do *teshuvah*, we are transformed, and so are our goals. What once seemed important is no longer important, because we are growing immeasurably as we move forward on the spiritual journey we have begun.

But there is much more to *teshuvah* than just deciding to change the direction of our lives. The decision to change is an indispensable first step, but in order to change we have to go beyond it. What do we do with our past? What about the people we have hurt because of the things we have done? Our deeds and their consequences do not disappear just because we express a desire to change.

Moses Maimonides, the great medieval philosopher, argued that *teshuvah* is an ongoing process. It is neither automatic nor spontaneous, and must be done in stages. Because *teshuvah* takes place in a series of phases, we are able to deal with our past over the passage of time.

We begin, says Maimonides, with regret for what we have done. A sense of regret can creep up slowly and deliberately, overwhelming us to the point of near-paralysis. Or it may take us by surprise, reminding us of what we have done when we least expect it. Often it smacks us right in the face without warning. Whatever form regret manifests itself in, we just don't feel right. We are uneasy. Maybe we can't sleep, or our appetite wanes. Or perhaps we seek solace by eating too much. In any case, we are uncomfortable but aren't exactly sure why. As a result, our acts become burdens lying heavily on our soul. This feeling of remorse motivates us to seek out the person we have offended and ask forgiveness. More than a simple "I'm sorry" is needed; we have to find out what we have done wrong and then try to do whatever will set things right.

Once that is accomplished, we are ready to approach God with our burden. According to Rabbi Moshe de-Trani, a kabbalist who lived in Safed in the sixteenth century, repentance is all about drawing close to God from the distance of sin. And sin beckons us all the time. It is the motivating force behind *yeridah*, the spiraling backward mentioned earlier. As Cain learned in the book of Genesis (4:7), sin lies couched at our door, ready to strike. No one is immune from it.

But don't let this deceive you into thinking that you can bypass the human interaction and go directly to God. Matters spiritual don't work that way. They take time. While God is central to the *teshuvah* process, and an approach to another human being is nearly impossible unless one has a relationship with the Almighty, we can only approach God after we have made amends with those we have wronged. And then we stand there, alone, desperately—often trembling with fear—waiting for divine judgment.

Our tradition advises, "Repent on the day before your death" (Pirke Avot 2:15). If you integrate *teshuvah* into your daily routine, your entire life will become part of the process of personal change. Once your life is realigned by means of the never-ending process of *teshuvah*, you will be ready to consider the other challenges discussed in this book

Knowing, Being, Doing

All first steps are difficult, but every journey must begin somewhere. Take the first step in the process of *teshuvah* by visiting the person you have wronged. If that isn't possible, phone or write a letter. There are no secret formulas, only honest contrition. You'll know what to do or say when you get there: whatever it takes to make amends.

Sometimes the people you might wish to approach are gone from your life or from the fabric of life itself. In such cases, we have to let go of the past in order to make room for the future, perhaps by building a new relationship with someone else.

More On Going Backwards/Making The Turn

Those who always walk on the straight path of righteousness feel no special pleasure in doing so, for they do not know that there is a crooked path. But those who begin on the crooked path and later find the direct path rejoice greatly. Similarly, the penitent appreciates righteousness more than the saintly person who never transgressed.

Dov Baer of Mezritch

I will heal their backsliding, I will love them freely, when my anger is turned away.

Hosea 14:5

The recognition of the need to turn comes about in different ways. Sometimes one is overcome by a sense of sinfulness, of blemish, of defilement, which results in a powerful desire for escape and purification. But the desire to turn can also take more subtle forms, feelings of imperfection or unrealized potential, which spur a search for something better.

Rabbi Adin Steinsaltz,
Teshuvah: A Guide for the Newly Observant Jew

There is a subtle art in formulating prayers of repentance. Because good and evil, sin and mitzvah are intermingled, one cannot pray for good as if goodness could be granted whole, a separate, distinct package. When the sages sought to pray that the powers of the *yetzer hara*, such as ambition, drive, and creativity be granted, stripped of their darker side, a voice from heaven informed them "they do not grant halves in heaven." The counsel flows from Judaism's reality principle. The wisdom of prayer and of penitence accepts the complexity and ambiguity of all power and urges the penitent out of love to squeeze the sparks of goodness out of the husks of evil.

Rabbi Harold M. Schulweis

Cast away all your sins with which you have sinned, and get yourself a new heart and a new spirit that you might not die, O House of Israel. For I do not want anyone to die, declares God. Turn you, therefore, and live.

Ezekiel 18:31–32

Those who have repented should not imagine that they stand far behind the righteous because of the iniquities or sins they have committed. It is not so; they are as beloved and precious to the Creator as if they had never sinned at all. Indeed, their reward is especially great, for despite having tasted sin, they have broken away from it and overcome their inclination to do evil. Accordingly the sages said, "In a place where the penitent stand, the completely righteous may not stand" (Babylonian Talmud, Berachot 34b). In other words, they stand on a higher rung than those who never sinned, because they have had to make a greater effort to subdue the impulse to do evil.

adapted from Moses Maimonides
Mishneh Torah, Hilchot Teshuvah 7:4

Is such the fast that I have chosen?
The day for a person to afflict the soul?
Is it to bow down one's head like a bulrush,
and to spread sackcloth and ashes under him?
Will you call this a fast,
and an acceptable day to Adonai?
Is not this the fast that I have chosen?
To loose the fetters of wickedness,
to undo the bands of the yoke,
and to let the oppressed go free,
and that you break every yoke?
Is it not to give your bread to the hungry,
and that you bring the poor who are cast out of your house?
When you see the naked, that you cover him,
that you do not hide yourself from your own flesh?
Then light will break forth from the morning,
and your healing will speedily come.

Isaiah 58:5–8a

When I kept silent, my bones wore away
through my groaning all day long.
For day and night Your hand was heavy upon me;
my sap was turned, as in the droughts of summer.
I acknowledged my sin before You and did not hide my iniquity;
I said, "I will make confession concerning my transgressions
   before Adonai"—
And You, You forgave the iniquity of my sin.

Psalm 32:3–5

A song of ascents.
Out of the depths I call You, O Adonai.
Adonai, listen to my cry;
pay attention to me,
to my plea for mercy.
If You keep account of sins, Adonai,
Adonai, who will survive?
Yours is the power to forgive
so that You may be held in awe.

I look to Adonai;
I look to You;
I await Your word.
I am more eager for Adonai
than guardians in the morning,
guardians for the morning.

O Israel, wait for Adonai;
for with Adonai is abiding love
and great powers of redemption.
It is You who will redeem Israel from all their iniquities.

Psalm 130

Rabbi Yose son of Rabbi Judah said: "A person who commits a transgression should be forgiven the first time, forgiven the second time, forgiven the third time, but not forgiven the fourth time, as it is said, 'Thus said Adonai: For three transgressions of Israel [yes], but for four I will not reverse it' (Amos 2:6), and 'Lo, all these things does God work twice, yes three times, with a person' (Job 33:29)."

Babylonian Talmud, Yoma 86b

Turning Toward Self

CHAPTER 2

Being a Boor/Becoming Human

Am Ha-Artzut/Menschlichkeit

Our masters taught that we may not ask an am
ha'aretz *to act as a witness, accept testimony from an*
am ha'aretz, *or reveal a secret to an* am ha'aretz; *we
may not appoint an* am ha'aretz *as guardian for
orphans or supervisor of tzedakah funds; and we may
not attach ourselves to an* am ha'aretz *on the road
[because of the danger of getting lost as a result]. . . .
Rabbi Eleazar added: By abandoning the Torah [and
its teachings], the* am ha'aretz *has no concern for his
or her own life, and therefore would have even less
concern for a fellow human being.*

Babylonian Talmud, Pesachim 49b

*For two and a half years, the schools of Hillel and
Shammai debated whether it would have been better if
humankind had not been created. They agreed in the
end that it would have been better had humans not
been created, but added that since humans have been
created, we should all examine our lives and determine
what we need to do.*

Babylonian Talmud, Eruvin 13b

W hat is a *mensch*? This Yiddish word (which literally means "human being") is heard quite often in English, at least as spoken by Jews. Sometimes we don't think enough about its real meaning. Kerry relates the following: "I can recall hearing my grandmother tell me to act like a *mensch* as she ushered me out into the world each day when I was a child. I don't remember ever asking her what the word meant, but I certainly knew what she meant when she used it—especially when she expressed it by describing a person who was not a *mensch*, the person I was not supposed to emulate. By using the term *mensch*, she was saying more to me than 'don't be a boor.' She wanted much more from me, much more from my inner sense of what is right and wrong, especially in terms of my actions toward others."

The virtue of being a *mensch* is difficult to define but can be illustrated by some examples of *menschlichkeit*, "humanness," as understood in Jewish tradition. Many of the positive *middot* listed in this volume would certainly make up part of the definition, but there are plenty of others, including kindness, thoughtfulness, generosity, and compassion, the very qualities most desperately needed in contemporary society.

Menschen, people characterized by the traits that comprise *menschlichkeit*, make the world a better place to live in. They are in demand by employers and by college recruiters. If more of us behaved like *menschen*, there would be less spiritual pain in the world, more kindness, and more personal integrity.

The great sage Hillel charged us, "In a place where nobody is acting human, strive to be human" (Pirke Avot 2:5). Hillel is here calling for something more than just an absence of boorishness; he is urging us to act decently regardless of how others act and regardless of the situation.

It is often difficult to step forward when personal courage is needed, but it is the simple acts, the routine stuff of which ordinary life is made, that make the difference in this world. That's where real heroism in the form of *menschlichkeit* can be found. As human beings we differ in a very important respect from the rest of God's creations. We have the ability, through our behavior, to alter our environment. By being a *mensch*, each of us can transform our own small part of the world and, by extension, ultimately every part of the world. As individuals, we have enormous potential to change ourselves and the world in which we live.

Elsewhere Hillel said, "Do not do to others what you would not want done to you." This rule provides an easy standard for measurement. Consider the impact of every action before you take it: how you would feel if the same thing were done to you? No one wants to be offended or hurt. Thus, Hillel's words provide a basic rubric for our actions, limits of which to be conscious, especially in cases where we cannot otherwise determine the consequences of our actions.

According to Rabbi Eugene Borowitz, the challenge of moral reasoning is to take cognizance of an action's consequences from word to deed. But beyond avoiding this baseline of damage, there is much good to be done by being a *mensch*. Each of us has the ability to extend ourself to another, to support one another's sojourn on earth, to nurture and offer guidance to others. Instead, we frequently ridicule and criticize, compete and actively search out occasion for others to fail, maybe even helping to facilitate their failures, so that we can jump in and take their place, gloating in our victory and the other person's defeat. A *mensch*, however, willingly supports others and is happy when they succeed.

Consider the story of Noah. The Torah states that "Noah was a righteous person in his time" (Genesis 6:9). Further on it tells us that Noah was by no means perfect. After bringing his family safely through the flood and ensuring the future progeny of the world, he stumbled and fell, as if he had totally forgotten how the human race had just been punished for its sinfulness and the world had come close to total destruction.

Centuries later, the rabbis reviewing this text were puzzled. Why would the Torah go out of its way to praise Noah despite his obvious shortcomings? Why was Noah deemed worthy to be saved from the great flood that washed the earth clean? The answer is that the Torah is praising Noah for being human. As one critic said, God has enough angels and too few *menschen*. But we are less like the angels and more like Noah.

When the rabbis read Genesis 6:9, they wondered whether the Torah was comparing Noah to everyone else in his own time, or whether it meant that Noah was so righteous that he would have been considered a righteous person no matter when he lived. They never resolved the question, but left it to us to figure out on the landscape of our own lives. We must assess ourselves in our own context.

While we may never formulate a definitive answer to this query, what truly matters is how we act at any given point in time. Through our actions, past is merged with present. Our past actions are often eclipsed by how we act today. We want to live a transformed existence. We want to become more and more resembling God's image.

The central lesson of *teshuvah* teaches us that we can all change, evolve, return—become better people. What really matters is not where we came from but where we are right now—and ultimately where we are going. With clear values in mind, with a sense of our ultimate goals, we must consider carefully how we act in the here and now.

The first step toward becoming a *mensch* requires a change in attitude. This is sometimes a major challenge. It has taken us years to frame the attitudes we have today. The far-reaching attitudinal changes required in becoming a *mensch* are not generally spontane-

ous. They develop over time and take work. Nevertheless, it is attitudinal change that will keep us moving on the upward curve.

Once we are able to move from the limitations and self-centeredness of boorish *am ha-artzut* and can reach outward to others
by being a *mensch* in the simple non-heroic acts of everyday life,
then we can advance further in our upward movement toward God.
Real change is measured by what we actually do and not by what we
merely want or intend to do. How we actually behave toward others, both those we know and love, and especially those whom we
don't know or don't love, is the only real measurement of *menschlichkeit*.

It is also a measure of one's relationship to God, for as Rabbi
Levi Yitzchak of Berditchev taught succinctly, the extent to which
one loves God can be measured by the extent to which one loves
others.

Knowing, Being, Doing

Make a difference in someone's life today by being a *mensch*. Plan
what you are doing to do and gather a sense of purposefulness to do
it, but be open to opportunities as they present themselves. Give up
your seat on the train to another. While in your car, let someone
turn in front of you. Don't honk the horn as soon as the light turns
green. Invite someone who seems to be in a hurry to go in front of
you on the supermarket checkout line. And don't forget to smile at
the toll collector and say thank you when handed your receipt. Say
hello to the letter carrier. Ask about the well-being of the bus
driver. Make their day a little brighter and our world a little better;
be a little more human.

More on Being a Boor/Becoming Human

> Rabbi Nehorai said: "If you humiliate another person, you will be
> humiliated in the end. Moreover, angels of destruction will thrust at
> you and expel you from the world, exposing your shame to all
> humanity."
>
> Desire a good name in divine service and in the love of all human
> beings for the honor of heaven, and not for your own honor and sta-

tion in the world, as those fools do, who desire a good name in the world for their own glory in the vanities of the world, and not for the glory of God.

Sefer Ma'alot Ha-Middot

Noah is known in Yiddish as a *tzaddik-in-peltz*—a righteous person in a fur coat. Why? Rabbi Menachem Mendl of Kotzk explained that if you are cold, there are two ways to get warm: you can heat the house or you can put on a fur coat. The difference between the two is this: in the first case the whole house is warm and everyone else feels comfortable, whereas in the second case only the person wearing the fur coat feels warm and the others continue to freeze. Some righteous people, when they see that Jewish observance is "cold," do everything possible to warm up the entire area. Other righteous people, however, isolate themselves in their own little space in order to ensure that they will not be swept along by the stream.

Ben-Azzai used to say, "Treat no one casually and think of nothing as useless, for everyone has his or her moment and everything has its place."

Pirke Avot 4:3

The Holy One said to Israel: "My children, what do I seek from you? I seek no more than that you love one another and honor one another."

Tanna d'Bei Eliyahu 26

"And the human became an animal being" (Genesis 2:7). Rabbi Judah said: "These words teach us that God first provided the human with a tail like an animal, but then removed it for the sake of human dignity."

Genesis Rabbah 14:10

Rabbi Judah said: "Every day we should say this blessing, 'Praised be the One who has not made me a *am ha-aretz*,' for an *am ha-aretz* does not fear sin. How may this be illustrated? By comparing it to a monarch who asks a servant who knows nothing about cooking to prepare a meal. The servant, not knowing how to cook properly, burns the meal and incenses the ruler."

Tosefta, Berachot 7:18

CHAPTER 3
_____

Overwhelmed by Depression/ Feeling Multiple Kinds of Joy
Dika'on/Sasson V'Simchah

Ten Rules for Achieving Joy, According to the Slonimer Rebbe

1. *Joy comes from studying Torah and giving satisfaction to your Creator, in accordance with your ability.*
2. *Joy comes from constantly probing your actions and regretting every unworthy act.*
3. *Joy comes from recognizing the aid your Master continuously gives.*
4. *Joy comes from reminding yourself at all times to fear Adonai and divine retribution.*
5. *Joy comes from devoting your life to study.*
6. *Joy comes from sanctifying the name of Adonai by your acts and taking care to avoid the opposite.*
7. *Joy comes from continuously increasing your devotion in the service of Adonai.*
8. *Joy comes from withstanding temptation.*
9. *Joy comes from serving with a whole heart and not considering such service out of the ordinary.*
10. *Joy comes from ending your days in repentance and holy service, and dying with a clear conscience.*

Or Yesharim

Our language has many words to express certain emotions that are central to the experience of being human. Joy is one such emotion. The sages of ancient times, we are told, used ten different Hebrew terms to describe its many different aspects; these are translated into English as joy, gladness, merriment, a ringing cry, leaping, exulting, a shrill cry, jubilation, a resounding cry, and shouting (Avot d'Rabbi Natan 34, Song of Songs Rabbah 1:4).

Every emotion, every form of joy, has its own special quality: a child leaping through a field of dandelions; a family dancing merrily at a wedding; Jews celebrating festivals with jubilation. Even with the knowledge that all human things are finite casting a shadow on our lives, joy is a potent force. It bursts through all the other emotions that claim our mood. It captures our souls. It lays claim on our hearts. While sadness has the potential to heavily burden us, joy is able to transform lives.

Our tradition connects the emotion of joy with the desire and need to express gratitude. Wherever joy is found, you will also find a sense of thanksgiving. When we overflow with joy, we are moved to thank God in a variety of ways.

Consider the Hallel psalms. Listen carefully the next time they are recited in synagogue or at a Passover seder. The prayer-songs comprising the Hallel reflect our feeling of gratitude to our Creator for so many things, a thanksgiving both individual and collective. If you open your heart to the words, their joy will overwhelm any sense of sadness you may have carried into the synagogue with you.

But expressing gratitude through joy is important not only when it bursts forth involuntarily, and not only when we feel like expressing it. In Judaism, joy is sometimes demanded of us. According to Rabbi Lawrence Hoffman, the Jewish holidays, during the course of the annual festival cycle, actually take us through the full range of emotions.

For example, on Sukkot, the fall harvest festival, the biblical verse which commands gladness at this particular time is applied: *V'simachta b'chagecha v'hayitah ach same'ach* "Rejoice on your festivals so that you might be happy." This divine instruction invites us to strive for joy at certain designated times of the year. It means that we can let go of any personal sadness when the tradition calls for joy, thereby providing the opportunity for a catharsis of sadness at a time like Tisha B'av, which commemorates the destruction of the Temple and the dispersion of the Jewish people.

The directive to be joyful means living in the moment and acknowledging its unique blessings. Every moment has a potential for joy and gladness. Some moments demand it, force it, inspire it; let us miss none of them.

The Babylonian Talmud (in Shabbat 30b) tells it this way: God so desires joy that the Shechinah, the Divine Presence, will be found, according to one text, only where there is joy. Some say that true joy only comes from serving God by fulfilling a mitzvah: "Then I commanded joy" (Ecclesiastes 8:15) refers to the joy of obeying a precept, no matter how basic or mundane. This should prove to you, say the rabbis, that the Divine Presence rests neither in the midst of sadness nor in the midst of idleness, neither in the midst of frivolity nor in the midst of levity, but only in the joy of actually doing a mitzvah.

The rabbis discuss this passage with reference to the prophet Elisha, whose power of prophecy left him whenever he plunged into a deep gloom. Once he was able to overcome his sadness, the ability to prophesy was restored. That music can prod the human emotions is inherent in its mysteries. That the human soul can be prodded is its mystery.

Another rabbinic text says that those who bring joy to the depressed (like a jester who makes people laugh, thereby pacifying those who are arguing with one another) will receive the highest reward, a place in the world to come (Babylonian Talmud, Ta'anit 22a).

Every human being is ultimately responsible for his or her own happiness. Nonetheless, even if you do not believe in the notion of the next world—or that we will receive a reward there, as the classical rabbis believed—it cannot be denied that each of us has a role to play in helping others to experience joy. Our relationships with one another provide a sacred opportunity to affect the emotional state of other people. How we approach the challenges of our own lives can inspire others to an emotional heroism which will carry them from the depths to the heights.

Judaism sees the relationship between the individual and God as similarly able to inspire the deepest joy and pleasure, as well as the strength necessary to ascend from the depths of despair. Here the psalmist cries out: "From the depths, I call to You. Listen to my cry; let Your ears be attentive to my plea for mercy" (Psalm 130:1–2). Calling out is a human need. Hearing human voices is God's delight.

Rabbi Abraham Joshua Heschel insisted that the core meaning of our existence is experienced in exaltation. Heschel taught that we must seek the greatest summits of joy merely in order to survive the mundaneness of life on earth. In his classic *Who Is Man?* he stressed that "The insecurity of existence lies in the exultation of existence. This is one of the rewards for being human: quiet exultation, capability of celebration. It is expressed in a phrase which Rabbi Akiva offered to his disciples: A song everyday, a song everyday."

Joy is connected to many other values discussed in this volume: God, faith, hope, Torah, interpersonal relationships, knowledge. It can penetrate our very being through every experience in the physical and social world. It can lead us gently like a baby's breath or with the kind of force that God used to create the world. But we will be guided, just with the simple act of putting out our hand and letting joy take hold of it. If we open ourselves up to joy and all its possibilities, even reach out for it and grasp it ourselves with our very being, then joy may find a means to dance its way into us.

Knowing, Being, Doing
Collect in your mind three memories of the deepest joys you have ever felt. Imagine that those who were present then are dancing around you now. Collectively, they all reach out, inviting you to join them in their circle. Reach out to them. Dance with them. Then go out and find the possibility of a new moment to be joyful and join in the dance.

More On Overwhelmed By Depression/Feeling Multiple Kinds Of Joy

Rabbi Israel Salanter taught that a true believer should never say, "It is bad," but rather, "It is bitter."

Rabbi Baruch of Mezbizh was once entertaining a distinguished visitor from the land of Israel. His guest was forever moaning the destruction of Zion and the fall of Jerusalem some two thousand years earlier, unable, even for one moment, to forget the sorrow of the Jewish people. On the eve of the Sabbath, Rabbi Baruch sang: "He who sanctifies the seventh day . . . " in his usual manner. When he came to the words "Beloved of God, you who await the building of Ariel," he looked up and saw his guest sitting there gloomy and sad. So Rabbi Baruch raised his voice almost to a shout, and sang right in the face of his startled guest, "Beloved of God! You who wait for the rebuilding of Ariel, on this holy day of the Sabbath, be joyful and happy!" Thereafter, the guest sang the song with joy to its end.

Another Chasidic rabbi once auditioned two cantors to sing for the upcoming High Holy Days. The first moaned as he intoned the holiday liturgy, audibly weeping. You could hear his sorrow in every word. The second cantor sang with great joy, smiling as he articulated each phrase. Everyone in the congregation was upset when the rabbi chose the joyful cantor. "You chose the wrong one," they complained. "The Holy Days are solemn and serious. This is Yom Kippur, when we are supposed to be solemn, not Purim, when we are supposed to be full of joy." As an explanation the rabbi told the following story: Once upon a time a king needed someone to sweep the palace floor. He tried out two janitors. One sobbed as he worked, bemoaning his sorry lot. The second sang as he worked, happy to be in such a wonderful place. The king chose the second janitor, explaining that it made him happy to be in the presence of so happy a person. The rabbi continued, "God feels the same way. Repentance is a holy act. On Yom Kippur, we sweep the sins out of God's chambers. It is holy work, to be sure. And there is great joy in doing holy work—even though it is serious."

When Adonai brought back the captives to Zion
we felt as if in a dream.
Then our mouths were filled with laughter,
and our tongues with song.

Even among the nations they said:
"What great things Adonai has done for them!"
Indeed Adonai has done great things with us!
How we rejoiced!

Adonai, bring back those who cannot return,
like streams in a dry land;
that those who sow in tears
may reap in joy.

A person who goes out weeping
carrying seed to sow;
shall come back singing
carrying the sheaves.

Psalm 126

Our masters taught: Do not say the Amidah prayer when depressed, indolent, laughing, gossiping, frivolous, or engaged in idle matters, but only when still rejoicing after the performance of a mitzvah.

Babylonian Talmud, Berachot 31a

Therefore, with joy shall you draw water out of the wells of salvation.

Sukkah 5:1

"The heart knows its own bitterness, even as with its joy no stranger can interfere" (Proverbs 14:10). What does this mean? That just as the heart is the first to feel distress when a person is anguished, so too it is the first to feel the joy when a person rejoices.

Exodus Rabbah 19:1

CHAPTER 4

Succumbing to Ignorance/ Acquiring Wisdom
Boorut/Chochmah

Do you know how Rabbi Akiva got started as a great teacher? Until the age of forty, he had no formal schooling. Then one day, standing by a well, he asked a companion, "Who hollowed out this wellstone?" His friend responded, "Akiva, haven't you read in the Torah that 'water wears away stone' (Job 14:19)? It was worn away by water from the well falling on it constantly, day after day." Akiva thought to himself, "Is my mind any harder than this stone? I will go and study Torah." So he went and studied until he learned the entire Torah.

Avot d'Rabbi Natan 6

How indeed does one acquire wisdom? One thing is clear: there are no easy formulas, no step-by-step methods. Kerry recalls the following: "My teacher, Jacob Rader Marcus, of blessed memory, and I used to have a specific time each day for drinking tea and eating cookies. We would work together early in the morning and then take a midmorning break. From him, I learned that wisdom is something quite different than knowledge or even learning. Wisdom is more than the simple accrued experience of years. And yet, his long life—he lived nearly one hundred years—combined learning, experience, and insight. It was he who taught me that facts can be memorized but wisdom must be internalized."

Many people experience life fully yet learn little. Some approach challenges as isolated events that have no relation to anything else. Our experiences might as well have happened to other people if we discern no connection between them. People who fail to acquire wisdom have little to offer others who may face similar difficulties.

How can we become wise enough to be able to help others with what we have learned? Especially when the others are our children or even our parents?

Wisdom comes from reflection, from experience, and from relationship. But it comes only when one repeatedly thinks about what one has learned—and then shares it with others.

Acquiring wisdom is an ongoing, lifelong activity. Like so many other things in life, it is never fully achieved. Recognizing this also takes wisdom.

At the same time, it is never too late to begin the pursuit of wisdom. In Jewish tradition, wisdom is acquired largely through the study of Torah, whose refracted light, the shining insights of generations of Jewish teachers, can illumine the soul. When you fully internalize the Torah, your face can glow with joy, as we are taught in Ecclesiastes: "Wisdom causes the face to glow" (8:1).

As a result, we realize that those who acquire wisdom have taken possession of a great treasure. The search for this treasure, which results in such a glow, is endless, but along the way it illumines many other things and other people. Slowly but steadily, its light enables you to see what was previously invisible.

Once you set yourself the goal of acquiring wisdom, just as Rabbi Akiva set himself to learn the whole Torah, the project you have undertaken will become important for reasons quite different from what you may have first imagined. This is because wisdom is linked to the soul's other spiritual aspirations, the quest to attain peace and to know God. On the other hand, without wisdom, the soul searches through a haze, faint with spiritual hunger, and is never sated.

Look at Joseph in the Bible. His experience is particularly poignant. It took Joseph many years and a great deal of personal anguish to acquire any measure of real wisdom. As a boy, he had a keen mind, but learned very little about himself, even from his dreams. He may have been intelligent, but he was not wise. He boasted to his brothers and father about how he would someday rule over them. Not something any parent or sibling would be eager to hear!

Joseph was not stupid. As Pharaoh's vizier, the highest-ranking official in Egypt, he reorganized the government and the system of land tenure. By judiciously providing for the future during the seven years of plenty, he enabled Egypt to survive the seven years of famine. But Joseph still played mind-games with his brothers when they came to Egypt to buy food. After he finally revealed his identity, he told them not to feel guilty for having thrown him into a pit and sold him into slavery. Everything that had happened, he said, was part of God's plan.

There was no anger or remorse. Once he understood that he had merely been a vehicle for God's work in the world, Joseph was no longer vengeful. While few of us are completely fatalistic, we all recognize that we often have little control over what happens in our lives. As a friend of ours recently quipped, "Someone is in control, but it ain't you or me!" That is real wisdom: a sense that there is a higher wisdom.

As we read in the midrash, "Kohelet taught that 'all the streams run into the sea' (Ecclesiastes 1:7). All of a person's wisdom is nowhere other than the heart. 'Yet the sea [read: heart] is not full' (Ecclesiastes 1:7), he went on to say. The heart of wisdom is never filled to capacity. One might think that if you let wisdom overflow from your heart by teaching another person, it will never flow back to you again. But Scripture says, 'Yet the streams flow back again' (Ecclesiastes 1:7)" (Ecclesiastes Rabbah 1:7).

To acquire wisdom, we must make ourselves into vessels which can receive knowledge as well as pour it out. Whatever we have learned we can teach. When we make ourselves into a vessel of this kind, we become transmitters of Torah.

In consequence of all this, learning and teaching Torah have become central Jewish communal activities. We believe that acquiring wisdom can be powerfully achieved not only in interactions between teachers and students but in *chevruta*, a dyadic study partnership between friends. That's why tradition teaches, "From my teachers I have learned a great deal, but from my students, I have learned most of all." (Babylonian Talmud, Ta'anit 7a)

Nevertheless, the ultimate absorption of wisdom into the heart and mind is something that happens on an individual basis. According to the medieval commentator Rashi, the Torah was revealed at Sinai to the entire Jewish people, but it was given to them as individuals rather than collectively. The Torah was revealed to each of the six hundred thousand persons standing at the foot of the mountain according to his or her ability and readiness to receive it.

Late in life, Rabbi Akiva came to understand that words of Torah can have a tremendous impact on the human heart. Yet words of

Torah, like the whole of Judaism, will have no effect if they are not seriously studied. So Rabbi Akiva began to learn, just as a child would begin its formal schooling, with the aleph-bet, all the while observing the world around him.

Each day Akiva would learn more and more, asking his teachers increasingly profound questions about the world of Jewish learning. His questions perplexed them more and more. Eventually they fell silent, unable to respond to the piercing insights of Akiva's mind.

Through perseverance and skill, Akiva slowly and steadily achieved what seemed impossible. Though a grown man, he transformed himself from a state of ignorance to one of the greatest Jewish teachers of all time. Such transitions, celebrated and modeled in our sacred sources, are still possible today.

Acquiring wisdom, as a Jewish ethical value, lies at the center of reflective human life. Unlike most of the other virtues discussed in the pages of this book, a conversation about wisdom is absent from many of the earlier collections of traditional Jewish texts on ethical virtues. These classic sources refer to acquiring wisdom largely in the context of seeking to know God through understanding and performing the *mitzvot*.

The idea of knowing God through seeking knowledge also reflects the teaching of the great medieval philosopher, Moses Maimonides, who suggested that knowledge of the world should lead to knowledge of God. This remains true in our time. Yet some of the mysteries of science have been revealed and used in ways that profane God's creation. Wisdom, like all qualities, is paired. It has a dark side. Wisdom can lead toward a meeting with God or away from it. The choice is ours to make.

Knowing, Being, Doing

Our masters taught: If you see a Jewish sage, say: "Praised is the One who has imparted divine wisdom to those who revere God." If you see a non-Jewish sage, say "Praised is the One who has imparted divine wisdom to God's creatures"

Babylonian Talmud, Berachot 58a

Prepare your heart for the study of Torah by reading through Psalm 119, which speaks of the Torah's importance. Then begin to study one chapter of Torah, one verse, or even one word. Begin anywhere. This week's Torah portion is always a good place to start. When you finish studying, you will be moved to say, "Oh, how I love Your Torah! All day it is my meditation" (Psalm 119:98). Then teach one idea, one word to a friend.

More On Succumbing To Ignorance/Acquiring Wisdom

Rabbi Elazar ben Azaryah said: "Where there is no Torah wisdom, there will be no good conduct; where there is no good conduct, there can be no Torah wisdom. Where there is no wisdom, there will be no reverence, where there is no reverence, there can be no wisdom. Where there is no understanding, there will be no knowledge; where there is no knowledge, there will be no understanding. Where there is no bread, there can be no Torah; where there is no Torah, there can be no bread."

He would often say, "To what shall we compare someone whose wisdom outweighs his deeds? To a tree whose branches are many but whose roots are few, so that, when the wind comes, it will uproot it and overturn it, as it says, 'One shall be like a tamarisk in the desert and shall not see when good comes; but shall inhabit the parches places in the wilderness' (Jeremiah 17:6). To what shall we compare someone whose works are more numerous than her wisdom? To a tree whose branches are few, but whose roots are many, so that, even if all the winds of the world were to come and blow on it, they could not move it from its place, even as it says, 'For one shall be as a tree planted by the water that spreads out its roots by the river. It shall not fear when heat comes, for its leaf shall be green. It shall not worry in a year of drought, for it shall never cease yielding fruit' (Jeremiah 17:8)."

Pirke Avot 3:17

The Baal Shem Tov taught that we read in the Talmud that forty-nine of the fifty doors to understanding were opened to Moses (Rosh Hashanah 21). But since humans always aspire to know more, how did Moses continue? When he found the fiftieth door closed to him, he substituted faith and meditated again on those phases of knowledge open to him. Thus, he taught, should we all discipline our minds. We should study and reflect to the utmost of our ability. When we reach the point where we are unable to comprehend further, we should substitute faith and return to the learning within our grasp. Beyond a certain degree, both the wise and the ignorant are alike.

Avoid the fool more than fire. For if you come moderately close to fire, you will enjoy it, but any degree of closeness to a fool is harmful. You will learn nothing from a fool, neither fear of heaven nor wisdom nor understanding nor appropriate conduct, but only vanity and folly. And it is for this reason that Solomon exhorted us: "Go far away from the person of folly, or you will not know the lips of wisdom" (Proverbs 14:7). A certain sage was asked, "What is your prime goal in life?" He answered, "To avoid fools."

Sefer Ma'alot Ha-Middot

What is the difference between a wise person and a fool?
Even fools say a wise thing now and then,
And the wisest sometimes descends to foolishness.
So what distinguishes a wise person from a fool?
A fool is one who never has a change of mind,
Conditions change, situations alter, and new times make new
    demands,
but the fool remains the same.

Rabbi Abraham J. Karp

God's presence, the Shechinah, is present when words of Torah are exchanged between two people.

Pirke Avot 3:2

Our sages said that this world is like the night. The dark of night has two effects upon us. We either see nothing at all or mistake one thing for another.

Moses Chaim Luzzatto

"And beyond wisdom, I have filled him with the spirit of God" (Exodus 31:3). Take the shopkeeper as an example. When a customer comes in to buy wine or honey or oil or fish brine, an experienced shopkeeper smells the customer's vessel. If it has been used for wine, the shopkeeper refills it with wine, and similarly if the vessel has been used for oil, honey, or fish brine. Likewise, when someone exudes an aroma of wisdom, the Holy One pours in more wisdom. Hence, "I have filled him with the spirit," implying that the spirit of wisdom had already been in him.

Tanhuma, Vayakhel 2

CHAPTER 5

Seized by Arrogance/
Giving Way to Humility
He-azat Panim/Anavah

Rabbi Simcha Bunam of Przysucha taught that we should keep two pieces of paper in our pockets, one saying, "For my sake the world was created," and the other, "I am nothing but dirt and ashes." Whenever we are overcome by feelings of pride, he said, we should read the paper with the words, "I am nothing but dirt and ashes." And when we feel as if our ego and sense of self have been decimated, reach into the other pocket and read, "For my sake, the world was created."

Since humility (*anavah*) is so important to Jewish religious life, one might expect the tradition to make a precise statement about it. But Jewish spiritual literature does not work that way. A definitive statement would prevent us from participating in the process of self-discovery and eventual change.

Our tradition recognizes that life's decisions are often not self-evident and require hard work. They demand constant self-scrutiny and inner struggle. Make no mistake about it: the work of personal repair demands a great investment of self. The quest for *anavah*, in particular, presents most of us with an ongoing challenge.

Humility is not a constant. It ebbs and flows. That is why we must be vigilant in our struggle to maintain it. Any definition of *anavah* demands a recognition that our spiritual world is in a state of constant flux. Humility is an attempt to achieve a balance between the tendency toward *he-azat panim*, haughty arrogance, and total annihilation of the ego, which the Chasidic tradition frames as *devekut*, a cleaving to God.

"From whence does our help come?" asks the psalmist, and responds, "Our help comes from God, the Maker of heaven and earth." But Chasidism was not satisfied with this. So it read the text a little differently. The phrase *me-ayin* is not understood as "from whence" but as "like nothing"; thus the psalm means that God's help comes when you make yourself like nothing and withdraw your ego. The Torah reflects the same sentiment.

There is a fine line between honest *anavah*, the soul-wrenching question of whether we are up to the task that God sets before us, and insecurity, the feeling that one is inadequate for the task. Some of us have egos so weakened by abuse that we are mere shells of self. Constantly in a state of motion as we move through life, we are responsible as individuals to seek to maintain the balance of humility in relation to the world as we experience it. Consequently, we are forced to change our perception of ourself as we confront the challenges and struggles of our everyday world. Yet we must always be mindful of the fact that we were created in the divine image (*bet-zelem elohim*).

While all of us have much in common with every other human being, and more immediately we are all part of the gene pool of our families, we are nonetheless unique as individuals. How we perceive ourselves in relation to others puts the essential religious principle of *anavah* into focus. As a midrash suggests, while coins that are minted from one mold are designed to be the same, God takes the human mold and creates from it a different person with each act of creation.

Our relations with others should be a reflection of our relationship with God. Martin Buber, the great philosopher/theologian, said that we should strive to raise all of our relationships to a level which reflects our ideal relationship with the Almighty. He called this special relationship "I-Thou" to distinguish it from more mundane relationships, such as those with objects, what he classified as "I-It." If we were able to reach the level of I-Thou in all our relationships—and this would demand constant effort on the part of both parties to the relationship—then we might be able to keep our sense of humility in balance.

Rabbi Eugene Borowitz, a leading liberal Jewish theologian, takes Buber's notion one step further. He argues that all of our relationships should be covenantal: they should all reflect the relationship established on Sinai nearly thirty-five hundred years ago. In that relationship, with God as our partner, there is no room whatsoever for arrogance, for all our egos are eclipsed in relation to the Almighty.

The rabbis of the talmudic era said it this way: "God cannot live in the same world with overly proud and arrogant humans. People should learn from what the Creator did when giving the Torah to Israel at Sinai. God paid no attention to the other high mountains and lofty peaks in the desert [which arrogantly wanted to be chosen]. Instead, God caused the Divine Presence to rest on Mount Sinai, a [humble] mountain which is not difficult to ascend. God's character is not like the nature of human beings," say the rabbis. "Humans most often pay attention only to those of the same (or higher) socioeconomic class, not those whom they consider socially or economically far beneath us. Yet God, who is exalted, takes cognizance of the lowly" (Psalm 138:6) [Babylonian Talmud, Sotah 5a].

Echoing this sentiment elsewhere in the Talmud, the rabbis suggest that whenever we find evidence of God's power, we also see evidence of God's recognition of humility (Megillah 31a). Thus, in all of our endeavors, we should model our lives on God's actions, as an affirmation of the covenant between us.

There are also those who believe that humility is not so flexible an ideal. For them, *anavah* is a constant. Arrogance of any sort has no place in this perspective. When seen from this perspective, attention to one's ego may get in the way of the striving for holiness in our lives.

Certainly there is much to learn from this. Some of us need to keep our self-centered egos in check at all times, particularly those whose station in life (because of money, power or influence) is itself lofty. Here Torah comes to remind us of a simple truth, "If you are arrogant, you will forget Adonai your God" (Deuteronomy 8:14).

Perhaps this injunction is intended for those who can't live in moderation, but only in the extreme. That's why the rabbis in Pirke Avot urge us, in their typically simple and straightforward style, "Just be humble in spirit" (4:4).

Knowing, Being, Doing

Bow your head and bend your knees in prayer, as our tradition suggests. It is one of the ways we humble ourselves in an effort to actively and constantly remind ourselves that God is above. This is also the reason why the tradition advocates keeping one's head covered while studying, at prayer, and during meals.

More On Seized By Arrogance/Giving Way To Humility

The arrogant are not accepted even in their own households. . . . The members of an arrogant person's family may begin by showing respect, but they end up finding find him [or her] repulsive.

Babylonian Talmud, Sotah 47b

Model *anavah* for the members of your household. For when you are humble and the members of your household are humble, and a poor person comes and stands in the doorway and inquires [of the children of the house]: "Is your parent home?" Even before the poor person has entered, a table is set for him. When he enters, he eats and drinks and then offers a prayer to God on behalf of the home-owner.

But when you are not humble and the members of your household are short-tempered, if a poor person comes and stands in the doorway and inquires [of the children of the house]: "Is your father [or mother] home?" they answer, "No!" and force the poor person to leave them.

Avot d'Rabbi Natan, Chapter 7

And thus did a certain sage say: "When people praise you for what you do not possess, worry and do not rejoice," and "When you see a person speaking of some good that you do not possess, be suspicious."

If you have acquired a good name by virtue of an excellence that you do not possess, do not let your heart swell, and do not take pride in yourself as if you had risen in that excellence. Do not crown yourself in it. But at least exert yourself to achieve the excellence that is attributed to you to exalt and glorify the Name [of God].

Sefer Ma'alot Ha-Middot

When Rabbi Judah passed through the city of Simonia, the townspeople asked him to appoint a judge and teacher for them. He selected Levi bar Sissi. The people built a platform for Bar Sissi to stand upon while addressing them. But when they came to him with their questions, he found that he could no longer remember the answers. Troubled by this strange problem, Bar Sissi rose early one morning and went to see Rabbi Judah. When Rabbi Judah saw Bar Sissi, he asked, "What have the people of Simonia done?" Levi bar Sissi replied, "They asked me three questions, but I was unable to remember the answers," then repeated the questions and answered them correctly. "If you know the answers," said Rabbi Judah, "why didn't you answer them when they were asked?" "They put me on a platform and on a tall chair. My spirit became conscious of the honor and the answers escaped me," replied Bar Sissi. "Let this be an example to all," commented Rabbi Judah. "When a person is filled with pride, wisdom escapes him."

Bereishit Rabbah 81

The most important of all worthy traits consists in behaving to the greatest extent possible with humility, modesty, and the fear of sin. Also, to the utmost degree, keep your distance from pride, anger, fussiness, foolishness, and evil gossip; and even if you have a good reason for behaving harshly, refrain from acting in that way. . . . Also, abstain from idle conversation . . . and do not lose your temper, especially with the members of your own household.

Isaac Luria

Rabbi Aaron of Starsola was asked how to become humble. He responded, "By fulfilling the *mitzvot*" and then added, "A tree rich in fruits is dragged down to earth by its fruits, and its branches hang downward. But a branch that is barren and withered stands upright without bending."

Priester das Liebe

We therefore bow in awe and thanksgiving before the One who is Sovereign over all, the Holy Blessed One. . . .

from the Aleynu prayer

With what shall I appear before Adonai and bow down before the exalted God? Shall I appear before God with burnt offerings or yearling calves? Will Adonai be pleased with thousands of rams, with ten thousands of rivers of oil? . . . It has been told you, O mortal, what Adonai requires of you: to act justly, to love mercy and to walk humbly with your God.

Micah 6:6–8

CHAPTER 6

Deceiving the Self/Building Integrity
Hashlayah/Shelemut

A psalm of David.
Adonai, who may stay in Your tent,
who may reside upon Your holy mountain?
One who lives without blame,
who does what is right,
who—in one's heart—acknowledges truth;
who speaks no slander,
who has never done harm to one's fellow,
or borne reproach for [acts against] one's neighbor;
for whom a contemptible person is abhorrent,
but who honors those who revere Adonai;
who stands by one's oath even at one's own cost,
who has never lent money at interest,
or accepted a bribe against the innocent;
the person who acts this way shall never be shaken.

Psalm 15

What psychologists call ego-integrity and moralists refer to as personal integrity is designated as *shelemut* in the Jewish tradition, from the root for *shalom*, meaning "peace" or "wholeness." Here we are talking about personal peace, inner peace, the cessation of internal strife, the solace of one's soul or inner calm. *Shelemut* is something that we all seek, especially in the constant clamor of the noisy, modern world. This value construct reflects a sense of the personal well-being and ego strength that enables us to confront the world and then retreat inside ourselves for respiritualization and renewal.

Shelemut does not imply a lack of inner struggle. Often, in fact, it is attained only as the result of a struggle. In fact, the struggle to attain *shelemut* is what *cheshbon ha-nefesh* (introspection) is—especially in preparation for the High Holy Days and other major life changes. And it all develops from coming to know oneself, after necessary interior strife, perhaps as part of the internal struggle.

By emphasizing this, Judaism demands that we do exactly what we are most likely to avoid. It demands that we scrutinize ourselves, that we examine ourselves carefully and constantly. *Cheshbon ha-nefesh* is an exhausting task, but without it we are unable to grow. Responding to this demand, difficult as it often is, is the means through which we develop personal integrity. Integrity does not mean living without flaw or failure. It means developing a way of life for yourself which reflects a depth of thought and feeling in accord with your conscience. Integrity also means not being afraid of what others might say, because you are confident in who you are and what you are doing.

Shelemut may sound like a rather simple idea, a rather straightforward goal. But often we spend so much time deceiving ourselves, pretending to be someone who we are not—through the clothes we buy, the houses in which we live, the cars we drive—that we dull ourselves to the essential self that was born into this world, the essential self that we may have hidden inside our soul in our zeal for "success."

And it takes time to recover that essential self, to peel back the layers that have accumulated over the years. Nothing of this spiritual height comes overnight. It takes hard work to know oneself, an understanding of one's strengths and weaknesses, and a willingness to work within (but also beyond) the parameters of that realization.

Recognizing this does not give us license to sit back and say "I can't do it," and then refrain from extending ourselves, from learning the requisite new skills required if we are to continue to grow. We need not live our lives trying to be someone other, but must use our knowledge of self to focus on what we can do well. We each have our own individual strengths that make us unlike anyone else. The challenge is to discover what we do well and to build our personal integrity in the process of doing it.

The psalm quoted at the beginning of this chapter offers us a point of departure. It states that the ultimate question of *shelemut* is not merely whether we can face ourselves or others, but whether we can go on to face God—whether we can approach God in the nakedness of self and abide by God's rules, subject to God's judgment.

The *Unataneh Tokef* prayer on Yom Kippur asks, "Who shall die by fire? Who by water?" and we might add, "Who by cancer, by automobile, by random acts of violence?" Through the piercing lens of the *Unataneh Tokef*, which forces us to take a good, hard look at ourselves if we are to avoid the ultimate reality of death for yet another year, we examine our deeds, the lives we lead.

Akavya ben Mahalalel, one of the early sages, put it another way: "Reflect on three things and you will not come into the grasp of sin: know where you came from; know where you are going; and know in whose presence you will have to make an accounting. Where do you come from? From a disgusting drop. Where are you going? To a place of dust, worms, and maggots. In whose presence will you have to make an accounting? The most Sovereign of Sovereigns, the Holy Blessed One" (Pirke Avot 3:1).

When you do not admit to these essential truths, you run the risk of deceiving yourself. Self-deception, a disintegration of self, leads to great spiritual pain. It also leads far away from a sense of shelemut.

Interpreting Psalm 15, Rabbi Jules Harlow asks: "Who may dwell in God's sanctuary? How can we merit a place in God's Presence?" He answers: "Live with integrity, do what is right, and speak the truth without deceit." Who indeed "may stay in Your tent; who may reside upon Your holy mountain?" Who among us may come before God feeling the least bit *shalem* (whole)? Perhaps we are all broken until we come before God. It is only in that coming forth that wholeness is possible. The people of Israel prepared for three days before the revelation at Sinai, but truly they had prepared throughout the journey in the desert of their lives. And it is only when we come before God after traversing the same desert that *shelemut* emerges as a possibility for us.

Knowing, Being, Doing

In the calm of an early morning or a late night, after you have showered or bathed and before it's time for make-up or a shave, look at yourself in the mirror. Spend some time peering into your own eyes. Are you comfortable in doing so? Or does anything you see make you uncomfortable? (When a child once asked what God looked like, Abraham Joshua Heschel advised him to look in the mirror.) Transcend the physical and ask yourself, "What have I become?" Is there anything you want to change? Choose one thing and begin working on it. Make the change. Next morning, look at the mirror again. Are you a little more comfortable? Just a little bit each day? Continue this process until you feel a sense of *shelemut*, of inner calm, swelling in your soul.

More On Deceiving The Self/Building Integrity

Know that the trait of deception is vehemently despised and abhorred by the Holy Blessed One. For to habitually deceive a friend is like killing that friend, as it is written: "As a deranged person who throws firebrands, arrows, and death. So is he who deceives his neighbor and says 'I was only joking'" (Proverbs 26:18–19). What's more, those who make a habit of deceiving their friends are certainly plotting evil against them, as it is written: "There is deceit in the heart of those who plot evil" (Proverbs 12:20). It is concerning this that King Solomon explicated his wisdom: "Do not plot evil against your neighbor; he [or she] is placing his [or her] trust in you" (Proverbs 3:29).

Those who begin by deceiving their friends will in the end lie to them. And if you habitually say things that are not true, it is like denying the Holy Blessed One, who is Truth. For falsehood is so called only in that it is not truth. And anyone who speaks falsely against a friend is, as it were, speaking falsely against the Creator.

Sefer Ma'alot Ha-Middot

Rabbi Papa was asked his name. He replied, "Rav Papa." The questioner chided him for having given his title as well as his name: "Doesn't the Torah tell us, 'Let others praise you, but not your own mouth' (Proverbs 27:2)?" Rav Papa replied, "Yes, but if there's no one else to do it, one must speak up for oneself."

Teshuvot ha-Rashba

The essence of *shelemut* is to join together two opposites. And don't be alarmed if you see a person who is in complete contrast to your mind (or your way of thinking) and you imagine that it is absolutely impossible to be at peace with that person; and also when you see two people who are indeed opposites (the one to the other); do not say that it may not be possible to make peace between them. on the contrary! The essence of the wholeness of *shelemut* is to attempt to make peace between two opposites, just as Adonai, the Holy

Blessed One, makes peace between fire and water, which are two opposites.

Rabbi Nachman of Bratzlav

The school of Shammai and the school of Hillel continually disagreed. What one forbade, the other permitted. Despite this, members of the school of Shammai did not refrain from marrying members of Hillelite families, and Hillelites did not refrain from marrying members of Shammaite families. This teaches us that even though they differed, they showed love and friendship toward one another, putting in practice the injunction, "Love truth, but also peace" (Zechariah 8:19).

Babylonian Talmud, Yevamot 14b

This is my prayer to You, my God:
Let not my spirit wither and shrivel
in its thirst for You
and lose the dew
with which You sprinkled it
when I was young.

May my heart be open
to every broken soul,
to orphaned life,
to every stumbler
wandering unknown
and groping in the shadow.
Bless my eyes, purify me to see
the beauty of humankind's rise in the world,
and the glory of my people in its redeemed land
spreading its fragrance all over the earth.

Deepen and broaden my senses
to absorb a fresh
green, flowering world,
to take from it the secret
of blossoming in silence.

Grant strength to yield fine fruits.
quintessence of my life,
steeped in my very being,
without expectation of reward.

And when my time comes—
let me slip into the night
demanding nothing, God, of humans,
or of You.

Hillel Bavli

Help us, loving Parent, to be able to go to sleep at night with a sense of wholeness and peace. Help us lie down in peace and awaken in the morning. Spread over us Your shelter of peace, guide us with Your good counsel, help us to live with integrity. Shield us from all the things in our lives which will destroy our sense of good. Remove all the evil forces that surround us, shelter us in the shelter of Your wings. You, O God, protect and deliver us. You are a gracious and merciful Ruler. Guard our coming in and our going out, grant us life and peace, now and always. Praised are You, Adonai, Eternal Guardian of Your People Israel.

adapted from the Hashkiveinu evening prayer

CHAPTER 7

Paralyzed by Anxiety/ Searching Out Tranquility

De'agah/Shalvah

Rabbi Nachman of Bratzlav taught that we should devote ourselves to meditation on our relationship with the Creator. In so doing, he advised, we are to judge ourselves by determining whether we have acted properly, and whether the things we have done are acceptable to God, who granted us life and is gracious to us at every moment. If we find that we have acted properly, we need fear no one, whether government officials, robbers, or wild beasts, and nothing in the world except Adonai. When we learn this, we will have attained, first, perfection in the study of Torah and in meekness; and second, perfect worship in which all personal considerations are forgotten; worship which asks no benefit for ourselves and prompts us to forget our very existence.

Likutey Etzot ha-Shalem

Most of life is not lived in a state of spiritual elevation or sunk below, hidden in a valley of shadows, but in a realm somewhere in between. Many people, interested only in life's peaks and assiduously seeking to avoid the valleys, turn to alcohol or other drugs. Tranquility (*shalvah*) is not found in either extreme, however. It is found in the miracle of the moment, in the beauty of everyday living, in the simple recognition of the miraculous complexity of the world, and of the lives we share.

The more we pursue tranquility, the more elusive it becomes. In fact, life is most tranquil when we don't work so hard at trying to achieve it. Our pursuit of *shalvah* may even prevent us from achieving it. That's part of the logic of Jewish spirituality.

Some of us only come to understand this bit of Torah wisdom as we grow older. It is among the hardest lessons life offers, especially in view of the pernicious seductions of contemporary society. Many people waste their lives and livelihood looking for that constant high, drawn in by illusions of power, influence, and authority.

Some of us, however, spend the substance of our lives on a plane that seems less exciting, even monotonous, to those who don't understand journeys of the spirit. The bulk of our years is spent following a routine of daily living, adjusted slightly as families change and the demands of work ebb and flow.

For the most part, our schedules vary little from week to week. Our jobs offer few of us much hope for the kind of adventure and excitement we may have dreamed about as children. Instead we worry (that's where *de'agah* comes in) about necessary material matters that seem of little import in the grand scheme of things.

At the same time, we watch our children gain independence and mold lives for themselves. While some people see this routine as boring and attach little meaning to it—too often running away during a so-called mid-life crisis—most of us realize that it is in the context of this stability that life can be lived most fully. Stability is, in fact, what gives life ultimate meaning.

The Gerer Rebbe taught that when he was a young man he wanted to change the world. By the time he reached what he thought was maturity (middle age), he wanted only to influence his community and those around him. In old age, he realized that all along he had been wrong. Throughout his life he had been looking in the wrong places, at the wrong things. All along all he needed to do was change himself. That's when the world around him seemed to change.

When we finally come to understand the positive aspects of living a balanced life, this approach to daily living can become a real goal. Then we will not worry about the anxiety that may once have plagued us. And as we grow toward that goal, we will find that the evenly balanced life can be raised in its entirety to a higher spiritual plateau.

Perhaps the balance between anxiety and tranquility, between *de'agah* and *shalvah*, is what the whole discussion of *middot* is all about. Recognizing that a series of drives are constantly pulling at us, we only need to find the place which allows us to live comfortably amidst each pair of *middot*, constantly adjusting for those times when we permit the drives to propel us as well as those when we need to regain control.

One of the reasons that the *middot* are usually offered in pairs, set as opposites in polar extremes, is that each moral virtue is generally best seen in relationship to its opposite. It would be easier to find the straight path if we were to consider only one aspect of our inner lives, providing us with an absolute way of living. But living a moral life is not so easy. We have to work for it, strive toward it, move on an upward spiral with it. Most of us do not live only in one extreme or the other. Instead, we live mostly between extremes, trying desperately to maintain a balance, to feel centered and thereby tranquil. Levi Yitzchak of Berditchev once saw a man running to his job, looking neither right nor left. "Why are you in such a hurry?" he asked. "I'm pursuing my livelihood," came the response. So Levi Yitzchak continued, "And how do you know that your livelihood is in front of you, where you can catch up with it? Maybe it's behind you, and you only need to stand still."

Once we determine the balance and tranquility of *shalvah* is our goal, how do we achieve it? Many Jewish rituals contain the potential to anchor our lives, mooring us to a place where we can steady ourselves amidst the waters of a storm-tossed sea.

The struggles and stresses of life, let alone death and disease, always threaten our balance. They make us anxious and cause us to worry. To counteract this, rituals of various kinds, reflecting the spiritual rhythm of the Jewish calendar, provide us with signs and symbols which can elevate us to a higher spiritual plane.

Take Shabbat, for example. As we leave work on Friday afternoon, anticipating the peace of the Sabbath, our bodies begin to slow down. As we distance ourselves from the workaday world, we become aware of our normal patterns of breathing once more. This is our life breath. We again become aware of the fullness of our lives and the decisions about real priorities that we have to make in them.

Even the simple act of lighting candles to usher in Shabbat each week provides us with a prism which enables us to glimpse a refracted bit of light from the next world. This does not happen just because we strike the match and ignite the flame. Our eyes have to be open to see the light.

Some rabbis suggest that we should make our lives like a desert, hearkening back to the formative years of the Jewish people, whose spiritual psyche was shaped in the desert sojourn from Egypt to Canaan. The desert calm provided our people with a context for spiritual development.

The Torah itself was given in the midst of total silence, perfect tranquility. Only the utterances of the Divine could be heard. Amazingly, many of us find it difficult to endure silence, inviting a television or radio to provide background noise and artificial companionship. We may not even pay attention to its chatter, but turning on the radio or TV (of course, only after listening to our answering machine) is one of the first things many of us do when we come home. Perhaps we long for noise because we have let the Sinaitic experience elude our memory. Let's try to bring the majesty of Sinai back into our lives, so that we will no longer require secular noise.

The dominant image of tranquility culled from Jewish tradition is embodied in the Shechinah, God's indwelling presence on earth. Here God can be experienced most keenly. We have the potential in the essential core of silence to invite God's presence into our midst. Wrapped in the wings of the Shechinah, much as we wrap ourselves in a tallit for morning worship, we can find tranquility and peace, *shalvah* and *shalom*, any place, any time.

Knowing, Being, Doing

Visualize God's ministering angels surrounding you. On your right is Michael, full of grace. On your left is Gabriel, strong and powerful. In front of you, filled with soft light, is Oriel. And behind you is Raphael, who brings healing to the soul. And all around is the presence of the Shechinah, a loving God.

More On Paralyzed By Anxiety/Searching Out Tranquility

Three things sap a person's strength: anxiety, travel, and sin.

Babylonian Talmud, Gittin 70a

Rabbi Hanokh told a story about a man who found it difficult to find his clothes in the morning. He was so upset that he was afraid to go to bed at night, fearing that he would not remember the next morning where he had put his things. One evening he decided to write down the exact location of each article of clothing as he undressed. He was very pleased with himself the next morning. He took his list and read "cap"—and there it was; "pants"—and there they were. As he reviewed the list, he located each item and put it on until he was fully dressed. "That's great," he said to himself. "But where in the world am I?" He looked and looked but could not find himself. "That's how it is with each of us," cautioned Rabbi Hanokh.

Rabbi Isaac of Akko taught that if you practice solitude in order to acquire the solitary state, so that tranquility will rest upon you throughout your life, you must adhere to three things and distance yourself from their opposites. If you do, you will have peace not only in this life, but also afterwards. The three things are: that you find satisfaction with your portion, that you love solitude, and that you remain free from arrogance and self-importance. To do so constitutes subjugation of the heart. The opposite of these feelings involves not being satisfied with what you possess and being bored when you are by yourself. Instead, you delight in the companionship of other people and their chatter; [likewise] you enjoy indulging in idle conversation and the pursuit of self-glorification and haughtiness.

Elijah de Vidas
Reishit Chochmah

It is extremely degrading to be a glutton and a guzzler, voracious and ravenous. For this trait is found only among the absolutely wicked, it being written in this regard: "Come, I will fetch wine, and let us guzzle strong drink. And as this day shall it be tomorrow— even more so!" (Isaiah 56:12). The throat is small in size but vast in capacity. Therefore, give it only what it needs. For if you give it many sweet foods today, tomorrow it will desire even more, and a small quantity will not suffice. But if you accustom it to scant, light fare, this will become natural to you, and you will not lust for fat foods and sweet delights. This is similar to what our sages of blessed memory have said: "There is an organ in each person [referring to the sexual drive], which if sated, hungers, and which if made to hunger, is sated" (Babylonian Talmud, Sukkah 52b).

Therefore, be circumspect in [avoiding] this base trait; do not habituate yourself to it, and content yourself with eating and drinking lightly, so that you may enjoy rest and tranquility without pain or illness while yet in this life of vanity, and so that you be reckoned among the righteous (as it says in Proverbs 13:25): "The righteous one eats to the satiety of one's soul."

Sefer Ma'alot Ha-Middot

I often left my family and friends and fatherland, and went into a solitary place, in order that I might have knowledge of things worthy of contemplation, but I profited nothing; for my mind was very tempted by desire and turned to opposite things. But now, sometimes even when I am in a multitude of people, my mind is tranquil, and God scatters aside all unworthy desires, teaching me that it is not differences of place which affect the welfare of the soul, but God alone, who knows and directs the activity howsoever God pleases.

Philo of Alexandria

Creator of peace, Compassionate God, guide us to a covenant of peace with all of Your creatures, birds and beasts as well as all humanity reflecting Your image of compassion and peace. Give us strength to help sustain Your promised covenant abolishing blind strife and bloody warfare, so that they will no longer devastate the earth, so that discord will no longer tear us asunder. Then all that is savage and brutal will vanish, and we shall fear evil no more. Guard our coming and our going, now toward waking, now toward sleep, always within Your tranquil shelter. Beloved are You, Sovereign of peace whose embraces encompasses Jerusalem, the people of Israel and all humanity.

Rabbi Natan Sternhartz
Lekutei Tefillot 1:95

Adonai is my shepherd
I lack nothing
God gives me my ease in rich pastures,
Leads me to take my drink by tranquil waters
Redeems my life
Leads me in the ways of right.
Out of sheer graciousness
Though I go through the gloomiest valleys,
I fear no misfortune, for You are ever with me,

Your sustaining staff is what relieves me of my anxiety.

My enemies do not bother me, because You are watching over
me.

You have made my heart fat with richness,

my cup overflows.

As long as I live my tracks will be accompanied by graciousness.

I will dwell in Adonai's house

as long as I live.

Psalm 23

CHAPTER 8

Exploiting the Body/
Protecting the Spirit
Zenut/Tzeniut

*All the other women bent over to gather ears of corn,
but she sat down to gather them; all the other women
hitched up their skirts, but she kept hers down; all the
other women bantered with the reapers, but she was
reserved; all the other women gathered from between
the sheaves, but she gathered only what had already
been abandoned—two sheaves, not three . . .*

Ruth Rabbah 4:6

*Rabbi Simcha Bunam once said: "We read in our
morning prayers, 'Fear God at all times, in private as
well as in public, and acknowledge the truth.' If someone asks whether you have performed a certain pious
act, do not modestly deny that you have done it. Avoid
ostentation in piety, and in everything you do, but if
asked, acknowledge the truth."*

Emet Kenah

"I'm not going to let ancient patriarchs dictate what I wear at my wedding," said the bride, quickly adding, "Their fashion statements are as time-bound as mine."

We often think of *tzeniut* (modesty) in terms of the body only and not the spirit. In its special, legal forms, it seems to be an antiquated idea formulated by men to define and confine women, to limit their dress and control their "naturally sexualized" behavior. This view is underscored when we reflect that Judaism's traditional moral literature was written by rabbis who saw the world through a male prism.

From the enlightened and egalitarian standpoint of the twentieth century, it is easy to conclude, from what they had to say on the subject of *tzeniut*, that the rabbis of talmudic times were consciously seeking to dominate women by regulating their interactions with others. Or perhaps they were attempting to rein in their own libidinal drives (framed as what they called the *yetzer hara*, an innate inclination to do evil) by placing limits on "others," particularly women. They also defined modestly somewhat circularly, for according to the Babylonian Talmud, they said that "anyone who fulfills the words of the sages is considered modest (*tzeniah*)" (Niddah 12a).

Whatever one's perspective on the past, an understanding of modesty requires much more than just a study of the historical restrictions on women's clothing styles. True modesty reflects an approach to behavior that shapes all of our interactions with others: man and woman. *Tzeniut* can also be a discussion of the spirit as much as the body, of spiritual modesty and not only physical modesty. *Tzeniut* is not just about whether a woman's legs or shoulders or hair (if she is married) should be covered.

The failure to understand the full dimensions and implications of *tzeniut* leads to the mistaken notion that it is about nothing more than revealed or concealed flesh. A synagogue usher once asked Kerry to do something about a young woman guest at that day's Bat Mitzvah celebration, whose dress revealed much more than the usher thought appropriate. Kerry gave her a tallit. What better way to cover her up than in God's glory! The fact that she talked incessantly during the worship service seemed not to bother the usher. He was more concerned about what she was wearing, or better said, what she wasn't wearing.

For man or woman, *tzeniut* is necessarily about our behavior (of which dress is only one aspect) within the context of defining who we are in our relationships with others than about covering up one's body to prevent others from being attracted to it, and—so goes the logic—seduced by it.

Our relationship to the culture in which we live is made clear by our clothing choices. We communicate who we are within a culture by the way we choose to dress. The relationship we have with our own body and how much of it we want to share with the world in a given context. Rabbi Camille Angel observes that it now seems popular to reveal whatever was kept hidden in the past (what we might call *zenut*), whether biographical, anatomical, or otherwise personal.

Thus, the notion of *tzeniut* demands that we reconsider much of what modern society takes for granted in regard to the exposure of body and, ultimately, soul. If the soul is housed in the body, then everything we do with our body is a reflection of our soul. One rabbi put it this way, "Always measure your actions as if the Holy

One were dwelling within you" (Babylonian Talmud, Ta'anit 11a–b).

At the very core of *tzeniut* is the idea of holiness, the separation between the holy and the potentially holy (the mundane, the common, the everyday). While the body is a housing for the soul, it is also what makes us human and therefore potentially sacred. We imitate God through procreation, utilizing our bodies in order to do so. But how we treat our bodies in everyday life and how we consider the bodies of others, covered and uncovered, determines whether they are, in our eyes, the beautiful creations of a loving God or simply objects of lust and desire.

To paraphrase a popular truism, we are what we wear. Furthermore, we are *how* we wear what we wear. And by extension, we are also the sum total of what we do in what we wear.

As autonomous beings, we are presented each day with numerous options, choices which provide opportunities to manifest our sense of *tzeniut* or the lack thereof. Certain types of clothing call attention to our bodies in ways that are appropriate to a specific time and place. Clothing can be complementary, enhancing our self-concept and self-esteem. Or clothing can tease others, sending out messages, blatant or subliminal, of sexual availability.

As a result, our choices of how to dress inform our behavior and on some level determine the behavior of others. We can hide behind our clothing, refusing to admit to ourselves or reveal to others who we really are. Or we may cling to the latest trends in fashion, buying specific brands "to fit in," revealing ourselves and making ourselves vulnerable in ways that we would not otherwise choose. Sometimes we use clothing to project an image, to show ourselves as that someone whom we want others to perceive us to be. In so doing, we may even deceive ourselves into thinking that's who we have actually become.

Clothing covers what is ideally only revealed in a loving sexual relationship. Such relationships are indeed holy when they reflect a sense of mutual respect and intimacy.

When we keep all of this in mind, we see that the rabbis of old tried to make things easy for us. By limiting our choices in clothing and "cover-ups," they sought to limit our opportunities to err. But by mandating our approach they also deprived us of the opportunity to struggle with who we are, to use our Jewish sense of self to inform our decisions about daily life. The rules they imposed deprive us of the possibility to use the Torah as a mirror in which we can see ourselves more clearly.

Ruth's behavior, as described in the midrash at the beginning of this chapter, was considered modest. She was conscious of the clothing she wore, how her body moved in her clothing, how she went about her work, how she acted with men she did not know, and how she integrated "Torah values" into her daily living, given her environment. Her modesty is best understood in her understanding of self and the choices she made as a result of that understanding. A modern-day Ruth might well do none of the things mentioned in the midrash, yet interact in her workplace in a way comparably modest, by the standards of our own time.

Clothing can also communicate the physical behavior we prefer. Liberal social norms generally do not reflect the recognition of self that Ruth displayed. Instead secular society allows for a variety of liberties, such as hugs and kisses between virtual strangers. How does conventional behavior of this kind impact our modern, more liberal consideration of *tzeniut*? Does it cause us to lose sight of how the body can be desecrated when it is touched in "unholy" ways?

With so much touching, held in check only by fears of litigation or contagious disease, we find ourselves struggling to define who we want to touch us and how we want to be touched, especially outside of our most intimate relationships. The ideology of political correctness emphasizes "personal space" and consciousness of sexual and physical abuse, but rarely are these ideas put in a context of the sacred. This is accomplished through the application of *tzeniut* in our lives.

While boundaries may be blurry and discomfort is often unconscious, this must be our goal. Without a sense of boundaries, it is often difficult to maintain a sense of the sacred. As we become sensitive to the psychological, medical, and legal implications of dress, behavior, and physical contact with others, we become able to examine how each affects our spiritual self.

Our bodies were created by God in a joint partnership with us. Therefore, as religious people, we believe that God, at least in some sense, "owns" our bodies. When we are able to understand ourselves in this greater context, when we truly love our bodies, we will have less of a need to assert our bodily presence. Instead we will be able to contract our need to have our body become public property. We can make room for communication between that is not based on another person's response to our body. In so doing, we will be able to honor our bodies to honor our Maker.

Knowing, Being, Doing

We dress each morning so as to stand respectfully before God. When you select your clothing and get dressed tomorrow, do so as if you were going to meet God. Because you are.

More On Exploiting The Body/Protecting The Spirit

Immodesty and obscenity are among the traits most despised and abhorred by the Holy Blessed One. For thus have our sages, of blessed memory, said: "If you sully your mouth with profane language, even if a propitious decree of seventy years has been sealed for you, it is transformed to evil, as it is written, 'Therefore, Adonai will not rejoice in your youths, and will not pity your orphans and widows. For all is flattery and wickedness, and every mouth speaks obscenity. Because of all this, Adonai's wrath does not turn back, and Adonai's hand is stretched out forevermore' (Isaiah 9:16)" (Babylonian Talmud, Shabbat 33a). Everyone knows why a bride goes to the bridal canopy, [to fulfill her sexual urge and join in sexual union with a man]. Everyone knows, but if you sully your mouth [by revealing the reason], even if a propitious decrees of seventy years [normal life expectancy] has been sealed for you, it is transformed to evil.

Sefer Ma'alot Ha-Middot

Using foul language is a grave transgression, and those who do so are despised by others for having ignored the decency and modesty that characterize the people of Israel. The person who does so follows the path of insolence and arrogance.

Israel Al-Nakawa, Menorat Ha-Ma'or

"And David danced before Adonai with all his might" (2 Samuel 6:14). Just what did he do? He dressed, say our teachers, in glistening garments embroidered with fringes shining like gold, and he struck his hands one against the other, clapping them. As he danced, crying, "Hail, exalted God!" the glistening gold fringes made a tinkling sound. Moreover, he pulled up his skirts, thus baring his legs, and cavorted as Israel cheered loudly, sounding horns and trumpets and all kinds of musical instruments. When he reached Jerusalem, all the women looked at David from rooftops and windows, and he did not mind. But Michal did not let him come into the house. Instead, she ran out into the street and pummeled him with reproaches, saying, "The king of Israel has certainly honored himself today, exposing himself in the sight of the servants of his subjects, just like one of the riffraff!" (2 Samuel 6:20). She went on, "What you have done today proves that my father's house was truly noble. Look at the difference between you and my father's house. Everyone in my father's house was modest and godly. While you— you stand and uncover yourself like one of the riffraff." David replied, "Am I acting up before a king of flesh and blood? And am I not acting up for the Sovereign who is Sovereign of Sovereigns? They of your father's house sought honor for themselves and put aside the honor of heaven. I do not do so; I seek the honor of heaven and put aside my own honor. Moreover, 'I will gladly be honored among the servants you speak of' (2 Samuel 6:22). Those daughters of Israel whom you call servants (*amahot*) are not servants, but matriarchs (*immahot*). Would that my share were with them in the time to come."

Numbers Rabbah 4:20

A disciple of the wise should do everything modestly: eating, drinking, bathing, anointing, putting on sandals, walking, dressing, bathing, speaking, disposing of spittle, even good deeds. A bride, while still in her parents' home, acts so modestly that when she leaves it her very presence proclaims: "Let anyone who knows of anything against me come and testify." Likewise, the disciples of the wise should behave so modestly that their very acts proclaim what they are.

Derech Eliayhu Zuta 7

Three things, says the Talmud, characterize the Jewish people: compassion, kindness, and modesty. Few liberal Jews today would feel uncomfortable with the first two adjectives, but the third is somewhat foreign. . . . "Modesty" perhaps evokes visions of Victorian repressiveness. Or the term might sound piously Puritanical—something the goyim do, not Jews. Or is it a hangover from the ghetto culture of Eastern Europe? Today, after all, we have discovered the virtues of all that is "natural"; and we are being taught by a variety of psychiatrists in best-sellers how to assert ourselves, how to "look out for Number One," how to stop being "modest" and cast away all sexual inhibitions, and so forth.

. . . The Torah tells us that what is "natural" for a human being is to be different from an animal. . . . It is natural for [hu]man to elevate himself, to perfect himself, to strive—even the most saintly and seemingly perfect [hu]man must continually do so, for as the Talmud says, "There is no rest for the righteous."

But neither does the Jew negate nature, the physical, the body: he refines and elevates it. . . . As the Hasidic saying goes, "God takes spiritual things and makes them physical, and Israel takes material things and makes them spiritual." . . . Precisely the realm of the mundane, physical raw material of nature is what the Jew elevates, sanctifies. And it follows that clothing, too, is not meaningless fabric—it, too, is an aspect of sanctification, an expression of the spirituality of the Jew.

It is important to note, however, that "sanctity" . . . is based on the sanctity of person, of life, the life of the body as well as the soul. The laws of *pikuach nefesh*, for example, the saving of life, superseded [almost] all other laws of the Torah, even though *pikuach nefesh* involves danger to the body. For the body, too is *kadosh*, holy [because we are created in the image of God]. . . .

Kedusha is one of the most important aspects of *tzeniut*; privacy," "modesty," are not expressions of contempt for the body, the physical, but on the contrary, expressions of their *kedusha*. A Torah scroll, for example, is covered, because of its high degree of *kedusha*. A woman's body—as well as a man's—is covered, because it is *kadosh*. [Modesty] . . . has not to do with just hemlines or headcoverings, but with thought, speech, sexual relations—our sense of who and what we basically are, a sense that our personhood is *kadosh*, inviolate. The body is not a piece of property, an object to be disposed of casually; it, too, is an integral part of the sanctity of personhood, the *kedusha* of the Jew.

Shaina Sarah Handelman, "The paradoxes of privacy,"
Sh'ma 9, no. 161 (Nov. 10, 1978): 2

What is really meant by modesty in dress? Does it mean that I should not wear a pants suit to work? Does it mean I should not appear on a public beach in a bathing suit? Does it mean that I should cover my hair? Can I wear sleeveless dresses? Handelman [quoted above] says that a person's body is covered because it is *kadosh*. Is my body less *kadosh* in a bathing suit than in a long dress? For me the question is not one of modesty in dress but rather appropriateness in dress. . . .

. . . In the area of sexuality, as in the area of dress, the major issue is one of appropriate response. It is appropriate in certain instances to "open up" emotionally, to touch or kiss or be physically intimate. In other situations it is inappropriate. Who is to judge? Each individual should be encouraged to make his/her own decisions based on his/her own understanding of the sanctity of personhood.

Rabbi Laura Geller, "Modesty is expressed in many fashions,"
Sh'ma 9, no. 162 (Nov. 24, 1978): 11

Reaching Toward Others

CHAPTER 9

Otherness/Created in the Image of God

Acheirut/Betzelem Elohim

Adam was created alone in order to teach us that causing a single soul to perish is like destroying the entire world, and saving a single soul is like saving the entire world. Another teaching: Adam was created alone for the sake of peace, so that we cannot say to each other: "My ancestor was greater than yours." We are all created from the dust of the earth . . . and none of us can claim that our ancestors were greater than anyone else's.

Babylonian Talmud, Sanhedrin 38a

Regarding the verse "God has made the one corresponding to the other" (Ecclesiastes 7:14), Rabbi Meir once said to Rabbi Elisha ben Abuyah who was known as "Acher" or "Other," "The Holy One created everything in this world with its analog: God created mountains, then created hills; God created seas, then created rivers . . . ."

Babylonian Talmud, Chagigah 15a

We were created *betzelem elohim*, "in the image of the Eternal," so says the Torah: "And God created Adam in God's own image" (Genesis 1:27). From the moment of Eve's creation, at which point the human species had two members, being human also implied a relationship between individuals. Thus, to be human requires an awareness not merely of self but of God and of others.

Because humankind was made in the image of God, God is the underlying factor unifying all of us with each other. Recognizing the relationship between ourself and others as a Jewish value construct is only part of the story. The self, even in its most ideal state, is not complete unless it actively interacts, or literally interfaces, with others.

The Torah clearly teaches what own life experiences affirm: We were not created alone, or to be alone. We are part of a larger community of human beings, whose presence in the world adds texture to our lives, individually and collectively. Because we know that we are not alone, we must always be aware of others as we attempt to understand the world and what it means to be alive. As a result, how we see ourselves is often dependent on how we see others and how others see us.

Only in the process of recognizing the "other" can we begin to understand what being human truly means. How we see others will also depend upon how we see God. In fully knowing another person, in recognizing that everyone else is also created in the image of God, we are compelled to seek a connection with others in order to unite with our Creator.

While we pray individually, for example, we generally do so together with other people in a communal setting. Certain prayers, in fact, may traditionally only be recited in a communal framework—a minyan, or prayer quorum, of ten adults.

Through knowing others and otherness, we come to better understand ourselves, and ultimately we approach the possibility of knowing the Creator of life and all selves.

In Jewish tradition, otherness begins in humanness. The first of the two creation stories in the book of Genesis tells us that Adam was created in contrast—in otherness—to the rest of creation. Unlike the earth, the stars, and all the other varieties of living creatures, God brought Adam into being alone. His sense of loneliness, of ultimate aloneness (the isolation and estrangement that constitute the human condition), was so acute that it demanded the creation of another human being, someone other and yet alike—Eve. Biblical Eve emerges not so that Adam will ever be understood as "same," but so that he can be understood, k'negdo (literally, "opposite him") in his otherness, and so that Eve as woman can be unique for her otherness.

Through much of Jewish history, the otherness of women made it possible to create a category which could be utilized to maintain a power structure in being female meant being less than being male. But the concept of otherness does not imply inferiority; it is only a way of indicating the existence of differences of certain kinds without valorizing them. Otherness, properly understood, leads not only to an affirmation of difference, but to a sense of God, and therefore a sense of likeness, of unity, for we all emerge from God and, whether female or male, we will all ultimately return to God.

As human beings, we all need an other as a necessary partner in reaching God, and therefore the other must not be pushed away or treated as less. In the other, you can glimpse God, perhaps even more powerfully than you see it in yourself. As Abraham Joshua

Heschel once said, when he wanted to see God, he looked in the face of a fellow human.

The other can also become the text of our own lives. Like Torah in this sense, the more we read it, the more our understanding of it deepens.

The most concrete attempt to unite with another human being is through sexual union. This may be why the Torah uses the euphemistic Hebrew word *yada* ("to know") to express sexual relations. In the intensity of sexual union, when it occurs in a committed loving relationship, we can briefly transcend the ultimate separation that sets each of us apart from everyone else.

The kabbalists—exponents of the Jewish mystical tradition—brought the imagery of sexual union into their view of the world, often using it to describe the individual's relationship with God. The *Zohar*, the classic mystical text, even teaches that the souls of lovers find their origin in the united soul that is separated into individuals at birth. From the moment of birth, they travel the universe until they find the original mate from whom they were separated.

The frustration of seeking but failing to achieve more than a few moments of ultimate union with another person reflects the disappointment we feel as we attempt to attain closeness to God, the Holy One of Being, eager to attain it yet understanding that intimacy with God (described as *devekut*, "clinging" or "cleaving") is never entirely possible. At best, we can only approximate it, come close to it.

Knowing this helps us to understand and thereby often to celebrate the "otherness" of the other. The contemporary theologian and philosopher Emmanuel Levinas summarized it best when he wrote that respect for the stranger (read: other) and the sanctification of God's name are strangely equivalent. Knowing and blessing another—an other—is a way of knowing and blessing God.

Knowing, Being, Doing

Look into the eyes of the person to whom you feel most closely connected. Watch the circles of his/her eyes spiral to a center of unyielding blackness. You cannot see further into the mystery of another person's being than that. Other people remain other to you no matter how much you know about them. The sense that you will never fully know another human being should help you to grasp the "unknowability" of God. But the more you know others, the more you see in them the image of God, invisible and impenetrable, the more you will know the mystery of God in yourself.

More On Otherness/Created In The Image Of God

Rabbi Joshua ben Levi said: "When a person walks on the highway, a company of angels go first, announcing, 'Make way for the image of the Holy Blessed One.'"

Deuteronomy Rabbah 4:4

Rabbi Akiva used to say, "Human beings are loved because they were made in God's image. This was made known to them by a special love, as it is said, 'For God made human beings in the divine image' (Genesis 9:6). Israel is loved because they are called children of God. This was made known to them by a special love, as it is said, 'You are children of Adonai your God' (Deuteronomy 14:1). Israel is [even more] loved because they were given a precious instrument. This was made known to them by a special love, as it is said, 'For I have given you a good doctrine, do not forsake My Torah'" (Proverbs 4:2).

Pirke Avot 3:14

To begin with oneself, but not end with oneself; to start from oneself, but not to aim at oneself; to comprehend oneself, but not to be preoccupied with oneself.

Martin Buber

One thing is necessary, of course, but only one: that men have a countenance at all, that they see each other. . . . The power to dissolve all that is rigid already inheres in the glance. Once an eye has glanced at us, it will glance at us as long as we live.

Franz Rosenzweig
The Star of Redemption

When a human ruler engraves someone's image on a wooden tablet, the tablet, it goes without saying, is larger than the image. Since God, the blessed Maker of worlds, is very great, God's image [the human species] must also be very great; the world [as the tablet on which the human image appears] is small, for humans, God's image, are greater than the world, [as is God] to whom it is said, "Adonai, my God, You are very great" (Psalm 104:1).

Exodus Rabbah 15:22

CHAPTER 10

Self-Centeredness/Performing Loving Acts of Kindness

Anokhiut/Gemilut Chasadim

One terrible winter night, a party of travelers headed by Rabbi Aaron of Karlin entered a village which had only one Jewish inhabitant. They went to the Jew's home and, without introducing himself, Rabbi Aaron asked for shelter, but the householder, having no idea who he was, refused. Words were exchanged between the rabbi's companions and the homeowner's servants, and when Rabbi Aaron finally revealed his identity, the homeowner asked him in. Said the half-frozen Karliner: "I see now why our sages say that it is more meritorious to extend hospitality to a fellow human than to God (see Babylonian Talmud, Shabbat 127). When the Shechinah finds the door to a house barred, she returns to heaven and no harm is done, except to the householder. With human beings, it is different; a person who is denied hospitality may perish.

retold by Chaim Bloch in *Gemeinde der Chassidim*

It's not always easy to extend oneself to another. There is so much in our own lives that requires attention and so little time to do all that needs to be done. Our days are consumed by obligations of work and family that leave us with woefully little time to reach out to others.

Fear of the stranger is also very real, especially in today's world, scarred by the increasing rate of random acts of violence. Indeed, what would you do if a stranger knocked on your door in the middle of the night, saying, "My friend has been hurt. Can you help?"

Doubtless you would pause, hesitate, fumble for a response that would allay the anxiety-ridden guilt bubbling to the surface. But you probably wouldn't open the door. So the stranger continues, "May I at least use your phone to call an ambulance?" Your suspicion does not subside. Fear threatens to overwhelm your sense of right. You mull over the options but still refuse to respond. All sorts of frightening things seem possible.

Are we so paralyzed with fear, so hardened by the accounts of savagery which fill the columns of our daily papers and the evening news reports, that we have become unable to help those in need? Acts of kindness, motivated only by a desire to help others, are part of the essence of what it means to be human, to be Jewish.

Anthropologists tell us that compassion is a uniquely human characteristic. This was well understood by the rabbis whose insightful statements are collected in Pirke Avot. They emphasized the importance of activism on behalf of others. As one of them said, "The [very existence of the] world depends on three things: Torah, worship (*avodah*), and loving acts of kindness (*gemilut chasadim*)" (1:2). Without these three factors, not only would humanity suffer, but the world itself would suffer and cease to exist.

The sages had more in mind than merely helping someone who asks for assistance. They were talking about much more than making a financial contribution to a worthy cause. While donating money is a sacrifice for many people, and adequate funding is indispensable to the maintenance of our communal institutions, giving money is relatively easy compared to other forms of *gemilut chasadim*.

Judaism demands much more of us than *tzedakah*. Judaism requires us to play a major role in repairing the world. According to tradition, God intentionally left the world unfinished so that we could help to complete the task begun in Genesis. To do this we must respond from the very core of who we are as human beings.

It is impossible for the self-centered to perform loving acts of kindness. You must, in fact, un-center yourself in order to act kindly toward another person. The rabbis charged us with the responsibility of caring for the world by reaching out in support of others, moving beyond the self and in doing so extending the self.

All human actions have consequences, and often they are predictable. The sages believed that every positive act leads to another and then to another. Similarly, undesirable behavior leads to further undesirable behavior. Good and more good until the world is transformed. *Mitzvah goreret mitzvah; averah goreret averah* "One mitzvah leads to another; one sin leads to another" (Pirke Avot 4:12).

When it is clear that a given behavior will lead to more good, or another to something less than good, the outcome may seem quite obvious. But the world rarely appears black and white, and choices are rarely so clear. Most of the time, we live in the gray area—the spaces in between clear choices, and as a result the moral decisions that face us are often fuzzy.

The fuzzier the world seems, the more difficult it is to take chances, because the outcomes are so unpredictable. Consequently, out of an intense need for stability and familiarity in an unstable and constantly changing world, we opt for the familiar, hoping that it will be the most predictable. This is how we find ourselves in the moral rut from which it is so difficult to ascend.

Yet every ascension, every climb upward from predictable, safe behavior to taking a chance, is accompanied by the possibility that it may have a positive effect on the world and on ourselves. Whenever we do the unusual, the incredible—giving money to a "street person" without questioning his or her need, opening one's door to an unfamiliar guest, visiting a stranger who is sick in the hospital—there is always the possibility of additional incredible acts occurring as a result: three more people take on the mitzvah of visiting the sick; the unfamiliar face soon becomes a family friend; a homeless person asking for a cup of hot coffee is not humiliated. One single act—your action—can transform reality.

Transforming reality, however, means challenging and changing the status quo—going beyond what is easy and predictable. We are pushing at what seem to be the limits of human behavior. Acting in this unusual manner is called *chesed*. The Bible records numerous examples of *chesed*: Boaz redeems Ruth and Naomi; Abraham welcomes weary travelers; a woman named Rahab in Jericho extends hospitality to two weary Israelites.

Chesed is one of the terms the Torah uses in describing God's attributes. It says, for instance, that God is the repository of extraordinary *chesed*: *Adonai, erech apayim v'rav chesed nose avon/* "God, slow to anger, abounding in kindness, forgiving iniquity" (Numbers 14:18). God shows unusual love and forgiveness, and whenever we go beyond the normally expected, predictable behavior, the more we are like God.

We become more like God when we act lovingly and kindly, when we do *gemilut chasadim*, because we are acknowledging that we can have an impact on the world when we extend ourselves beyond the usual and expand into other realms of behavior. The possibility of doing this is inherent in every action at every moment.

According to the messianic tradition embedded in our sacred sources, the world may be redeemed at any moment. And we must be prepared. The person you shove aside or, better yet, welcome into your home may very well be the Messiah.

Similarly, one may die at any time, God forbid. And for this too we must always be prepared. The tradition tells us to repent on the day before we die (Avot 2:10), but since we cannot know when we will die, this means that we must always be in a state of penitence. Every act of *chesed*, every attempt to stretch beyond the accepted limits of behavior, expands and improves the self.

The philosopher-theologian Martin Buber put it another way. He believed that all of our relationships should reflect the relationship we strive to build between ourselves and God, what he called an "I-Thou" relationship, as distinguished from I-it relationships of a less intimate, rather insignificant level. I-it relationships are not limited to interactions between humans. Buber believed that people are not obstacles on the path to the Divine. They are the path itself, and it is because of their relational nature that the tradition calls these acts "loving" acts of kindness. They take us toward others; and, as a result, toward God. This is how the rabbis of the Talmud phrased it: "The whole worth of a benevolent deed lies in the love that inspires it" (Babylonian Talmud, Sukkah 49b).

Some people like to consider *gemilut chasadim* as voluntarism, the uncomplicated act of giving one's time to a worthy cause. But a definition of this kind limits the Jewish perspective on doing loving acts of kindness. By doing such acts, we actually become the channel through which God's work is done in the world, or a "holy vessel" (*klei kodesh*).

The Lelover Rebbe said, "If someone comes to you for assistance and you say to him, 'God will help you,' you become a disloyal servant of God. You have to understand that God has sent you to aid the needy and not to refer him back to God."

As a result, we become partners in the ongoing work of maintaining the world. A contemporary Hebrew folk lyric says it all: *"Ani v'atah nishaneh et ha-olam* "You and I can [will] change the world." When we focus our energies on others and not on our-selves, the work we do can actually change the world. But when we are focused on ourselves, we are far from doing God's will; we are far from others, and, as a result, will ultimately regret our selfish-ness—moving furthermost from our most ideal selves.

While the self must rise to a higher level and expand in order to do deeds of *gemilut chasadim*, it must also contract, doing what the mystics call *tzimtzum*, in order to make room for the other person for whom we want to make space in our home, in our lives, in our hearts.

Chesed demands that the self expand and contract at one and the same time. This was true of God as well when God created the world. There was an expansion of God in actively creating the world with all its life-forms and complexities; and at the same time, Jewish sages have taught, there was a necessary *tzimtzum* on God's part in order to make room for the world to come into existence.

As this tradition indicates, God had to accept no longer being the entirety of the universe, but made room for the world and its inhabitants. The same holds true for us: we need to accept that we are not the center of the universe and make room for others to be at the center. Paradoxically, the more God contracted, the more God's presence could be known through creation; and the more we make room for others, the more they are aware of us.

Knowing, Being, Doing

Spend tomorrow doing *tzimtzum*, making room for others in your life. Try not to be the center of your world. Step back from control-ling conversations, from being aggressive and demanding in the marketplace, and allow things to develop around you and in you. Retract, contract from the world, and distance yourself a bit from your daily reality. Just for a day. Then, the next day, consciously plan an act of *gemilut chasadim* and see how much more possible it is because of what you did the previous day. Now imagine how many more acts of *gemilut chasadim* might flow from your initial act. How else can you improve the world even as you go about your business? How are you changed by acting this way? How is the world changed?

Try making a list of things you do that are *gemilut chasadim*. Sometimes you can plan to do such things by scheduling volunteer time in places like a soup kitchen or nursing home. Opportunities abound. However, in many cases, acts of kindness defy the very nature of scheduling. Don't let your daily planner come to be a scheduled program of self-oriented activities. The opportunity to reach out to others cannot be programmed into your day the way other activities may be. Plan to be present and act to ease the burden of others.

More On Self-centeredness/Performing Loving Acts Of Kindness

By opening your hand to the stranger, he becomes your brother. Jewish solidarity forms the basis of the fraternity of all Jews. Being Jewish requires seeing other Jews as fellow Jews. Our obligation is to realize in life that which is already a reality through God. A mitzvah is the translation of God's vision into human reality.

Reuven Kimelman

If a poor person who is unknown to you comes forward and says, "I am hungry; give me something to eat," do not suspect a deception and respond with questions aimed at uncovering it. Instead, feed the poor person at once.

Moses Maimonides
Mishneh Torah, Hilchot Matanot Anayim 7:6

Abraham . . . would go forth and make his rounds, and wherever he found travelers, he would bring them to his house. To the one who was accustomed to eating wheat bread, he gave wheat bread to eat. To the one who was accustomed to eating meat, he gave meat to eat. To the one who was accustomed to drinking wine, he gave wine to drink. Moreover, he built stately mansions on the highways and left food and drink there so that every traveler stopped there and thanked God. That is why delight of the spirit was vouchsafed to him. And whatever one might ask for was to be found in Abraham's home.

Avot d'Rabbi Natan 7

Rabbi Eleazar said: "Loving acts of kindness are greater than charity, for it is said, 'Sow for yourselves according to charity, but reap according to your lovingkindness' (Hosea 10:12). A person who sows cannot be certain there will be a harvest to eat from, but a person who reaps will surely have that which to eat." Rabbi Eleazar further said, "The reward for charity depends entirely upon the measure of lovingkindness in the act, as it is said, 'Sow for yourselves according to your charity, but reap according to your lovingkindness.'"

Babylonian Talmud, Sukkah 49b

Our sages taught, If you love your neighbors, befriend your kinfolk, are affectionate to a sibling's child, and lend money to someone in need, you are the type of person Scripture is speaking of when it says: "When you see the naked and cover him [or her] and do not hide yourself from [the needs of] your own flesh . . . then, when you call, Adonai will answer; when you cry out, God will say, '*Hineini*, I am here'" (Isaiah 58:7, 9).

Babylonian Talmud, Yevamot 62b–63a

CHAPTER 11

Gossip / The Ecology of Words
Lashon Hara/Lashon Hatov

Rabbi Jonah ben Abraham Gerondi taught that there are six forms of evil speech. The first is speech that criticizes others even when they are not at fault; this embraces the evils of falsehood and slander. The second is speech that criticizes faults that others really have; it is wrong, even though the criticisms are valid, not only because it harms the victims but because the speaker enjoys harming them. The third is the spreading of harmful tales that inflame hatred. The fourth is saying things that induce others to say evil things. The fifth is the use of unclean language. The sixth is speech that continually finds fault with others even when they mean no harm.

Words are powerful and unyielding. Once uttered, they live a life of their own. And words do many things. They can move people to act. They can provoke revolutions and change whole societies. They can grant freedom or sentence someone to death, they can uphold or deny human rights. With words entire nations are created or destroyed. And with words peace can be declared.

The Bible's undying influence is just one example of the power of words to change human history. Whether written or spoken, words provide the foundation for all significant actions. The world itself was created by words—spoken by God. The words of an Abraham Lincoln, a Martin Luther King Jr., a Theodor Herzl still ring in our ears; they continue to move us long after they were first spoken.

But what about our common everyday speech? It may not be the stuff out of which civilizations are founded, but simple everyday words also have the power to build up and tear down. They too can desecrate or celebrate, attack or defend. Too often, we hurl words without bothering to see where they land or what effect they have.

Thoughtless words have enormous potential to hurt; they can damage and destroy. And once words leave our mouths, it is impossible to retrieve them. This point was graphically illustrated by a famous rabbi. Assembling his followers, he ripped open a pillow and waved it in the air. The feathers floated upward in all directions. It was impossible to catch them. The feathers, the rabbi explained, are the unthinking, often inadvertent evil words we speak. There is no way to retrieve them. So you have to make sure not to utter them in the first place.

As children we were all taught, "If you have nothing nice to say, don't say anything at all." Jewish tradition goes one step further: Don't say anything about anyone; that way, there's no chance of saying something bad.

All talking about others, no matter what form it takes, is gossip, talebearing, and therefore potentially destructive. The prohibition against gossip, *lashon hara* (literally, "an evil tongue") stems from the verse "You shall not go about as a talebearer among your people" (Leviticus 19:16).

Our heritage has always emphasized this prohibition. The rabbis of the talmudic era, in fact, maintained that evil speech was like leprosy or a plague. The Bible condemns evil speech as lying or deceit. Although it does not use the term *lashon hara*, it often refers to its opposites, *lashon hatov* ("sanctified speech") and *lashon marpeh*, a healing or wholesome or good tongue, as in "A wholesome tongue is a tree of life" (Proverbs 15:4). Conversely, an evil tongue is a source of death.

Whenever we talk about others, we run the risk of engaging in evil speech. By gossiping, we figuratively kill a part of the person we are talking about. "Why is gossip like a three-pronged tongue?" ask the rabbis. "Because it kills three people at once: the person who says it, the person who listens to it, and the person about whom it is said" (Babylonian Talmud, Arachin 15b).

Lashon hara is the subject of a famous book by Rabbi Israel Mayer Kagan entitled *Chafetz Chayim: Shmirat Lashon*. Rabbi Kagan believed that the ability to express our thoughts is one of God's greatest gifts to us. Speech, he said, is not inherently evil, but everything we say must be guarded, guided, and well-intended. Taking care about what we say is not popular in twentieth-century America. Instead we try to be spontaneous, to cast off our repressions, so that we can express ourselves fully and "communicate" with others. Freely flowing words are supposed to be the means of compensating for all the harm that has been worked on our psyches throughout our lives.

Being circumspect and letting it all hang out seem to be in a fierce tension with each other. The two approaches are contradictory, but we must seek to achieve a balance between them, combining a modern psychological understanding of the self and of the importance of self-expression with a traditional understanding of the damage caused by speaking irresponsibly and without concern for others.

The effort to achieve this synthesis is exemplified in our day by a small group of people, most of them Orthodox, known as *shomrim* ("guardians"). They continually study the teachings about *lashon hara* and for two hours each day refrain from saying anything that might harm anyone else. One of their leaders is Rebbetzin Samet, a well-known teacher who lives in Jerusalem. She says: "If we care very much about someone else, we become creative in finding ways to avoid speaking *lashon hara*." Furthermore, and this holds even for those we do not know but might speak about, "It may be a sacrifice to keep quiet, but it is a small suffering compared to what these people are going through, having to bear the pain of what others say about them."

Knowing, Being, Doing

For two hours every day, refrain from talking about other people—the lowest level of speech. During this period do not speak with anyone to whom you habitually gossip. If necessary, simply do not talk at all, so as to prevent temptations and opportunities to gossip from arising. In order to strengthen your resolve, cultivate an awareness that you are preventing pain and perhaps even saving a life. Invite a friend or two to join you and support each other's commitment "to guard one's tongue."

More On Gossip/The Ecology Of Words

Rabbi Simcha Bunam once set out on a journey with a group of Chasidim. Around noon they arrived in a town. The innkeeper invited them to join him for lunch. While Simcha Bunam sat at a table, his companions went into the kitchen to see whether the food was kosher. Suddenly a man dressed in rags appeared and said, "You make a big deal about what you put into your mouths. Why don't you care as much about the things that come out of your mouths?"

Rabbi Ishmael taught that the biblical verse "Do not go out as a peddler among the people" (Leviticus 19:16) refers to the peddling of an evil tongue. Rabbi Nehemiah added: "Do not be like a peddler who transports gossip from one person to another, and the second person's gossip back to the first.

Jerusalem Talmud, Pe'ah 1:1

What constitutes *lashon hara*? Rabbah said: "It is like when someone announces that the oven at so-and-so's house is blazing hot." Abbaye asked: "What harm does that do? The speaker is only providing information." "Yes," said Rabbah, but information that is true may be uttered with the intent to do harm, as if the speaker were saying, 'Where else would the oven be so hot except in the house of so-and-so who has plenty of meat and fish?'"

Babylonian Talmud, Arachin 15b

The spies that Moses sent into Canaan said: "We came to the Land . . . and surely it flowed with milk and honey. . . . But the people there are fierce" (Numbers 13:27–28). This shows what slanderers are like; they begin by saying nice things and end with evil language.

Tanhuma, Shelah 17

We find in the Aggadah that slanderers hang by their tongues in Gehinnom because they spoke evil about their neighbors and transgressed the Torah's prohibition: "Do not go talebearing among your people" (Leviticus 19:16). Those who slander their neighbors by alleging that they have committed certain offenses are destined to succumb to the same offenses. We learn this from the example of Joseph. It is written: "And Joseph brought an evil report of them to their father" (Genesis 37:2). Our sages of blessed memory explain: "He would tell his father 'Your sons eat flesh torn from a living animal, they denigrate their half-brothers, the sons of the maidservants, by referring to them as slaves, and they lust after the maidens of the land' (Jerusalem Talmud, Peah 1:8). Joseph himself stumbled into all three of these sins! In regard to the first, the Holy One said to him: 'You say they eat flesh torn from a living animal? Even when they go astray [in selling you] they do not eat without ritual slaughter, as it is written: 'And they slaughtered a young goat' (Genesis 37:31). As for the second, you say they denigrate the sons of the maidservants by referring to them as slaves? 'Joseph was sold as a slave' (Psalms 105:17). Third, you say they lust after the maidens of the land? I shall incite 'the bear' against you," as it is written: 'And the wife of his master lifted her eyes to Joseph' (Genesis 37:13). What is stated there? 'And they could not speak to him in peace' (Genesis 37:4)." The very things about which Joseph disparaged his brothers are actually grounds for praising them, for they did not say one thing with their mouths and a different thing in their hearts.

Sefer Ma'alot Ha-Middot

Who is the one who desires life, and loves many days, that he may see good?

Keep your tongue from speaking evil and your lips from speaking deceit.

Depart from evil and do good; seek peace and pursue it.

Psalm 34:13–15

CHAPTER 12

Inclining Toward Evil/Doing Good

Yetzer Hara/Yetzer Tov

Rabbi Moses of Coucy, who lived in the thirteenth century, wrote, "It is because human beings are half-angel, half-brute, that our inner life witnesses such bitter struggles between such unlike natures. The brute in us clamors for sensual joy and vain things; but the angel in us resists and strives to make us know that meat, drink, and sleep are only means whereby to keep the body strong so that we can study truth and do God's will. Not until the very hour of death can it be certain or known to what extent the victory has been won. The one who is only beginning to live with reverence for God will do well just to say on rising, 'Today I will be a faithful servant of the Almighty. I will be on guard against wrath, falsehood, hatred, and conflict, and will forgive everyone who offends me.' For whoever forgives is forgiven in return; hard-heartedness and an unforgiving temper are a heavy burden of sin."

W e have to struggle to say or do the right thing. It's not that we don't know the difference between right and wrong—we do know. Yet, for some reason, we often choose to do what is wrong.

So what difference does it make? If you are not already familiar with the phenomenon of moral struggle, pay more attention to the inner self described by Moses of Coucy. It seems as if we are always grappling to find our essential self, even when we are not fully aware that there is a battle raging in the lower depths of our soul.

Sometimes, when we have to make a split-second moral decision, the process of weighing the consequences of our actions feels painfully slow. At other times, we just have gut feelings about whether something is right or wrong without really knowing the source of our "instinctual" moral sense. This sense is a measure provided by God, who is the foundation for the moral, the good, what is right in the world.

According to the rabbis, no matter who we are, no matter how good or bad we appear to be, two basic inclinations drive us: the *yetzer tov*, or "good" drive, and the *yetzer hara*, a drive that is not good, and often is so bad that the rabbis call it "evil." Like life itself, this rabbinic system for understanding the human psyche is far more complicated than appears on the surface. It is not a simple choice between good and evil or even between right and wrong.

That would make moral decision-making rather straightforward, but in reality moral reasoning is by no means so simple.

The concept of *yetzer tov* and *yetzer hara* accepts good and evil as coexisting in the world. These two opposing forces are continually fighting for dominance in our souls, in our lives. This does not mean that we have to excise the *yetzer hara*, and in fact that would be impossible, which is exactly the point the rabbis are trying to make. We must not delude ourselves into believing that we can ever be free of our negative impulses, our inclination to do evil. They are part of the essential ingredients that make us human and imperfect rather than perfect and fully God-like.

Our eyes may gaze into the heavens—and well they should—but our feet stand firmly planted on the ground. That is what it means to be human. As we all know from personal experience, human beings are capable of both good and evil. In light of this, and given what we have done to the earth and each other, the rabbis of the Talmud once discussed the question of whether or not the human race should ever have been created. The majority concluded that it was probably not one of God's better ideas. However, said the rabbis, since the human race has been created, we have to strive to be all that we can be, given our limitations and the struggle seething within us. (See Eruvin 13b in the Babylonian Talmud for the entire discussion, including the minority opinion.)

Consider the well-known story about Zusya of Hanipol? As he lay on his deathbed, he considered his impending appearance before God on the day of his final judgment. Zusya was not afraid of death itself and accepted God's decision that his days on earth were about to end. He was not concerned that God might ask him, "Why were you not like Abraham or Moses?" No, that did not frighten him. Instead, he was concerned that God might ask, "Why were you not more like Zusya?" Indeed, why are any of us not all that we know our essential selves capable of being? Yet becoming the best we can be is not possible until we are fully aware of who we are.

The rabbis certainly understood the predicament posed by the human condition. They understood the forces within their own bodies. The drives and desires. The inner forces that sometimes seem out of control. The good inclination and the evil inclination, to use their terminology.

Whoever we are, we all come from the same Creator. Our goal must be to harness our "evil" drives in order to transform their energy into a desire to do good. When properly harnessed, our *yetzer hara* can drive us forward to create, to achieve, to compete, to excel, to succeed, and even to do mitzvot.

While the sexual drive is everpresent, we can move from raw lust to a profound longing to bring children into the world, to shelter and nurture them, and then to guide them into a mature adulthood. "Without the *yetzer hara*, a human being would never marry, beget children, build a house, or engage in trade" (Genesis Rabbah 9:7).

When we keep our drives balanced, we will see that the *yetzer hara* is not evil in itself but only potentially.

Knowing, Being, Doing

List those things you have done in the past month that were motivated by the worst *yetzer hara* tendencies within you. Now list what you did that was motivated by a higher will, the drive of *yetzer tov*. Finally, list what you plan to do in the coming month to nourish that aspect of yourself.

More On Inclining Toward Evil/Doing Good

Rabbi Ammi said, "The *yetzer hara* does not slink along the side of the road. It walks boldly in the middle. As soon as it sees someone making eyes at someone else, hair all done up and walking with a swagger, it says, 'That one is mine.'" Rabbi Avin added: "If you indulge your impulse to do evil when you are young, it will end up your master in old age, as it is said, 'If you are too kind to a young servant, the servant will end up as master' (Proverbs 29:21)."

Genesis Rabbah 22:6

Rabbi Isaac said: "The impulse to do evil renews its potency every day, as it is written, 'Every impulse wrought his mind was sheer evil every day' (Genesis 6:5)." Rabbi Simeon ben Lakish said: "Our impulse to evil grows in strength from day to day and seeks to slay us, as it is said: 'The wicked watch the righteous and seek to slay him' (Psalm 37:32). If not for the Holy One's help, you would be unable to withstand it, as it is said, 'Adonai will not leave you in its hand' (Psalm 37:33)."

Tanhuma, Bereishit 7; Avot d'Rabbi Natan 16

"The end for darkness is set" (Job 28:3). A definite time was set for the world to spend in darkness. As long as the *yetzer hara* remains in the world, darkness and thick darkness are also in the world. After the evil impulse is pulled out of the world by its roots, the end for darkness will have been set.

Genesis Rabbah 89:1

When God came to create the world and revealed what was hidden in the depths and disclosed light out of darkness, they were all wrapped in one another. Therefore, light emerged from darkness, and from the impenetrable came forth the profound. So, too, from good issues evil and from mercy issues judgment, and all are intertwined: the good impulse and the evil impulse.

Zohar III, 80b

Woe to the wicked, who follow the dictates of their hearts and eyes, which deceive the body in sinning and drive their souls from the world. For thus have our sages of blessed memory said, "The heart and the eye are the two agents of sin—the eye seeing, the heart desiring, and the body going and doing" (Jerusalem Talmud, Berachot 1:5). This is what was meant by Moses, peace be upon him, when he taught: "And do not go astray after your hearts and after your eyes" (Numbers 15:39). And thus did Solomon say in his wisdom: "Give, My child, your heart to Me, and your eyes shall heed My ways" (Proverbs 23:26). That is, if you give Me your heart and your eyes and keep them from sinning, then your entire body will be guarded from transgression. This will make you Mine: the evil inclination will not prevail over you.

Sefer Ma'alot Ha-Middot

"My child, give Me your heart . . . and let your eyes observe My ways" (Proverbs 23:26). Why did the Holy One deem it necessary to ask Israel to direct their hearts and eyes toward God? Because transgression is dependent on these organs. Hence it is written, "That

you do not follow your heart and your eyes" (Numbers 15:39). The
eyes and the heart become the agents of sin.

Numbers Rabbah 10:2

Do not say, "God made me sin,"
for God does not make that which God hates,
and do not say, "God made me stumble,"
for God has no need of evil persons.
Rather, Adonai hates evil and abomination
and keeps them far from the pious.
From the very beginning, when God created humankind,
God gave us power over our will.
If you desire, you can keep the commandment,
and it is wise to do what God desires.
Fire and water are poured out before You.
Stretch out your hand to the one you desire.
Life and death are before humankind.
What you want, that will be given you.

Ben Sirach 15:11–17

What is the difference between a good and evil person?
There is some goodness even in the worst.
And is there a person who has not sinned?
So, what makes one person good and another evil?
An evil person refuses to change—
Doing wrong, knowing it,
And yet persisting in evil ways.

Rabbi Abraham J. Karp

CHAPTER 13

Abuse of Power /
Expressing Compassion
Aritzut/Rachmanut

*"This is my God whom I will glorify" (Exodus 15:2).
Abba Saul construed* ve-anvehu *["whom I will glorify"] as* ani ve-hu *["whom I am like"]. Hence, as
God is gracious and compassionate, so you are to be
gracious and compassionate.*

Babylonian Talmud, Shabbat 133b

*"Adonai, Adonai, a God compassionate and gracious,
slow to anger, rich in steadfast kindness, extending
kindness to the thousandth generation, forgiving iniquity, transgression, and sin" (Exodus 34:6–7). Just as
God is called compassionate and gracious, so you must
be compassionate and gracious, freely giving of yourself.*

Sifre to Deuteronomy 49

Compassion is a divine attribute seated within the core of the human soul. *Rachmanut* ("compassion"), or *rachmonis*, as those of our immigrant grandparents or great-grandparents who were of European, Yiddish-speaking stock might have said, is derived from the Hebrew word for "womb" (*rechem*). This suggests that expressions of true compassion emanate from the same place where the seed of human life is found, hidden deep within the human body.

Many consider *rachamim* to be rooted in the feminine side of our souls. In our longing to be Godlike, we yearn to procreate: to give birth and thus extend parental love to our children.

But our imitation of God extends beyond biology and is not restricted to our offspring. We are most like God when we show compassion to others. As it says in the *Zohar*, the classic mystical work: "If you are compassionate to a poor person and renew his [or her] soul, it shall be counted as if you had indeed created that soul" (*Zohar* II, 198a).

Opportunities to be compassionate present themselves every day as we interact with the world around us. Dr. Ellis Rivkin used to speak kindly to inanimate objects. Kerry found this habit rather silly until Dr. Rivkin explained, "If I treat things kindly, then I am more likely to be compassionate to others. This keeps me in practice."

In order to be compassionate, we have to open ourselves to others and respond with our hearts. Too often we are so self-absorbed that we fail to see opportunities to be compassionate, or fail to act on them if we see them.

The rabbis teach that even God may be tempted not to be compassionate. Just as we pray, they explain, so too does God. But what is God's prayer? "May My attribute of compassion overcome My attribute of [harsh] justice" (Babylonian Talmud, Berachot 7a). Rabbi Eleazar once said, "Even when angry, the Holy Blessed One still remembers to be compassionate" (Babylonian Talmud, Pesachim 87b).

As humans, we know that it is easy to strike out at others, to react without thinking and quickly pounce on them when they err or fail, especially those whom we love.

Compassion must extend to ourselves as well. Integrated into the cycle of the Jewish calendar are periods of forgiveness and compassion which allow us to take our tiny, insecure souls and move through the most difficult days.

We have to learn to forgive ourselves, to treat ourselves gently, even in the course of a healthy discipline. If we are not merciful with ourselves, it will be difficult to be merciful with others. Compassion for ourselves in our personal struggles will enable us to begin to understand and be compassionate toward others in their struggles.

Knowing, Being, Doing
Be kind. For everyone you know is fighting a difficult, and often different, battle.

More On The Abuse Of Power/Expressing Compassion

We have been taught that Rabban Gamaliel quoted in the name of Rabbi Judah the Prince: "God will turn from the fierceness of divine anger and show you mercy and have compassion on you" (Deuteronomy 13:18), and said, "Heaven is compassionate to those who have compassion for God's creatures. But heaven is not compassionate to those who have no compassion for God's creatures."

Babylonian Talmud, Shabbat 151b

Rabbi Jacob Isaac of Przysucha, known as the Yehudi and also as the Yud, and Rabbi David of Lelev, the Lelever Rebbe, called upon a wealthy man to ask for a charitable contribution. The man looked at the Yud, who was rather solidly built: "I won't give you a thing. If you want money, go to work." After they left, the man's neighbors told him who had been at his door. He ran out and apologized, and, of course, gave them a larger sum than he would have offered in the first place. When he asked to be forgiven, the Yud replied, "You didn't know who I was, so you haven't offended me. But you did know that I was a 'Yud,' and the common Jew within me cannot forgive you since you are not asking forgiveness from him. Show me by your future conduct that you respect the everyday person and you will thereby gain my pardon."

When the Kotzker Rebbe used to tell this story, he added that within every Jew is a common person and a higher inner person, both made in the image of God.

Kotzker Ma'asiot

"And when he [Moses] went out to look upon his brethren, he saw their burdens" (Exodus 2:11). How did he feel when he looked upon them? As he looked at their burden, he wept, saying, "Woe is me for your servitude. Would that I could die for you!" Since no work is more strenuous than that of handling clay, Moses used to shoulder the burden and help each worker. Rabbi Eleazar, the son of Rabbi Yose the Galilean, said, "He saw heavy burdens put upon small people, and light ones on big people; men's burdens on women, and women's burdens on men; the burden an older person could carry placed on a youth, and the burden of a youth on an older person. So Moses would from time to time step away from his retinue and rearrange the burdens, pretending that he was really trying to be of help to Pharaoh. The Holy One said, 'You left your own concerns and went to look compassionately at the distress of Israel, behaving like a brother to them. So, I, too, will leave those on high and those below, and speak [only] with you.'"

Exodus Rabbah 1:27–28

Rabbi Alexandri said: Two donkey drivers who hated each other were walking on a road when one of the donkeys collapsed under its burden. The other driver saw this but continued on his way. But then he reflected: "Doesn't the Torah say, 'If you see the donkey of one who hates you lying flat under its load and [your inclination is to] refrain from raising it, you must nevertheless raise it with him' (Exodus 23:5)"? So he returned, lent a hand, and helped his enemy to rearrange the load. He began talking to his enemy: "Loosen it a bit here, pull a little tighter here, unload over there." Before long peace developed between the two of them, so that the driver of the unloaded donkey reflected, "I thought he hated me, but look how compassionate he was." By and by, the two entered an inn, ate and drank together, and became friends. What caused them to make peace and become friends? Because one of them kept what was written in the Torah. Hence, "You have established harmony" (Psalm 99:4).

Tanhuma, Mishpatim 1

The Tzortkover Rabbi, David Moses, said, "If you obtain the compassion of your fellow, you will also obtain the compassion of God. For the angels of mercy argue, 'Surely the All-Compassionate One will be merciful to someone on whom a mortal has taken pity.'"

CHAPTER 14

Refusing to Help/Giving Righteously
Kamtzanut/Tzedakah

The sages taught that deeds of love are greater than tzedakah in three ways. First, tzedakah is done only with money; deeds of love, both with money and with one's person. Second, tzedakah is only for the poor; deeds of love, for both poor and rich. Finally, tzedakah is only for the living; deeds of love, for both living and dead.

Babylonian Talmud, Sukkah 49b

One Shabbat morning, a worshipper dozed off during the sermon while the rabbi was talking about the shewbread, the loaves of bread placed on the altar of the ancient Temple in Jerusalem. The congregant, nodding off and barely awake, sleepily imagined that it was God who was speaking. So that Friday morning, obedient to the command he thought he had heard, he took a dozen loaves of challah, placed them in the ark of the synagogue, and went home.

Shortly afterwards, the *shammes* of the shul stood in front of the ark, pouring his heart out: "Please, God, I don't even have enough money to buy food for Shabbat. If only You would help me, dear God!" The *shammes* opened the ark to kiss the Torah scroll—and out came tumbling a whole bunch of challah loaves. Naturally he assumed that God had responded to his plea, and uttered appropriate thanks.

Later that day, when the congregant arrived for evening prayers, he peeked into the ark to check on his "shewbread." Lo and behold, the challahs were gone! The *shammes* had put aside two loaves for his own Shabbat use and sold the rest in the market, using the proceeds to purchase other necessities, except for a few coins given to *tzedakah*.

This routine went on week after week for several months, without either man knowing about the other, until the rabbi happened to observe what was happening. At first, he wanted to tell each of them what was really happening and chide them for their foolishness. Then he realized that this was one of the ways that God works in the world, and he kept silent.

While some may argue that *tzedakah* is really just a fancy Hebrew word for charity—"the right thing to do"—it goes beyond the simplicity of giving small amounts of money or food for charitable purposes. *Tzedakah* is a distinctive way of approaching the entire landscape of sacred giving. It extends beyond tossing a few coins into a beggar's hand as you walk the city's sidewalks, hoping that he or she will go away and leave you alone and not use it to buy alcohol or drugs, or writing a check for your favorite cause as you sit at your desk and pay your bills each month, bombarded by requests for financial assistance and tax-deductible giving.

Tzedakah is a way of responding to the seemingly arbitrary and unequal way wealth is distributed. Today's heroes—movie stars and sports figures—gain fortunes, while those who make the world a better place often have to struggle to make ends meet. The real heroes, according to poet Danny Siegel, are those who make the world better by giving of their funds and of themselves to others in need.

Regardless of how rich or poor we may be, we are all obligated to give *tzedakah*—to redistribute some of our money. This fact teaches an important moral message: there is always someone less fortunate. We give to others as an expression of thanksgiving to God for what we have, no matter how little it may seem. We give to others as an acknowledgment that we are bringing the holiness of God's loving generosity to our shattered and impoverished world.

Seen this way, *tzedakah* is a way of participating in *tikkun olam*, repairing what is broken. "Rabbi Eliezar would give a coin to a beggar and then begin to pray. He explained this practice by quoting Psalm 15:15 'Through *tzedakah* shall I see Your face'" (Babylonian Talmud, Bava Batra 10a). Kerry has a wealthy friend who gives to many causes, but each of his gifts is anonymous. He tells only Kerry. Knowing that he has helped someone who needs help is all the satisfaction he needs.

Judaism teaches that there is no real ownership in this world. The structure of the Hebrew language gives voice to this notion. In Hebrew, you cannot say, "I have such-and-such." You can only say, "There is a such-and-such to me . . . [for this limited period of time that I am in possession of it]." In other words, we don't really own things, we are merely stewards of property during our lives and for greater or shorter periods of time.

Rabbi Irving Greenberg said it this way, "*Tzedakah* means taking responsibility for life. One shares one's own possessions in order to take responsibility for the needs of others because life is indivisible. My life cannot be whole while others' lives are not."

When we leave this earth, someone else is given the burden of responsibility. The biblical writer Kohelet fully understood this idea. *Tzedakah*, which has the same root as *tzedek* ("justice"), is a way of pursuing justice by using what resources we have to make the world a bit more fair. God created the world, but left it unfinished. In doing so, says the midrash, God made us partners in creation. *Tzedakah* is one of the many ways we are obligated to help finish the job by improving upon the world as we have found it, and as we wake to find it everyday.

Rabbi Samuel Kaminker related the following story: "I once resolved to devote a whole day to reciting the Book of Psalms. As evening approached, I was nearing the end. Around that time, my rabbi, Moses of Tzidnov, sent his assistant to get me. I asked the assistant to tell the rabbi I would come as soon as I had finished reciting the psalms, something Rabbi Moses and I had both agreed would be spiritually enriching for me. But the rabbi's assistant admonished me to come immediately. So I gathered up my things and went. When I arrived, Rabbi Moses of Tzidnov asked, "Why didn't you come when you were first asked?" I proudly explained the reason. "I spent the whole day studying the psalms, contemplating their application to my spiritual life. I was nearly finished when your assistant arrived." To this, Rabbi Moses responded, "I called you to make a *tzedakah* collection for an indigent Jew. Psalms can be chanted by the angels, but only humans can help the destitute. *Tzedakah* is a greater duty than chanting psalms, since the angels cannot perform the mitzvah of *tzedakah*."

Knowing, Being, Doing

Always keep a few coins or a granola bar handy as you walk down the street, in case someone in need asks for your "spare change" for food. While some of those you help may use what you give them for other than noble purposes, a generous response may help to restore a person's dignity and in addition provides food. And remember, our tradition suggests that the Messiah may be hiding in our midst. Perhaps his is the open hand extended to you.

If you have any pocket change at the end of the week, put it into a *pushke* (*tzedakah* container) just before you begin your preparations for that foretaste of the world-to-come, Shabbat. Because this aspect of *tzedakah* will ultimately affect the world, through the good work performed by the charitable organization that receives your donation, it will imbue your Sabbath rest with a sense of a world a tiny bit closer to being whole.

More On Refusing To Help/Giving Righteously

Our hearts often yearn to do charitable acts, but the evil impulse within us says, "Why give *tzedakah* and diminish your resources? Don't give to strangers, give to your children!" But the good impulse prompts us to do *tzedakah*.

Exodus Rabbah 36:3

Rabbi Abba said in the name of Rabbi Simeon ben Lakish, "Lending money to a poor person is greater than giving *tzedakah*; and putting money into a common fund to form a partnership with a poor person is greater than either."

Babylonian Talmud, Shabbat 63b

There are several things for which no definite amount is specified: . . . one of them is *tzedakah*. But this only holds when you do *tzedakah* with your person; when you do it with money, a specific amount is required.

Jerusalem Talmud, Peah 1:1

There are four approaches to giving *tzedakah*. Giving it willingly but not wanting others to give is grudging toward others. Not giving oneself but wanting others to give is grudging toward oneself. Giving willingly and wanting others to do the same is pious. Finally, not giving but wanting others to give is wicked.

Pirke Avot 5:16

Sublime, inspiring, exceptional, extraordinary, uplifting, wonderful, incredible, ineffable, unique, warm, great, lovely, exquisite, caring, loving, sensitive, awesome, amazing. Again and again these words and similar combinations of them appear in the telling and re-telling, the writing and re-writing of the nature and workings of *tzedakah*. The inner essence of *tzedakah* flows freely in a universe of human acts and encounters that do, I believe, inspire, amaze, and leave both participants in the act and observers moved, to tears, to joyous dancing, to amazed, dumbfounded whispers. An idea-made-real that summons up such lyricism points to other strings of words: hope, trust, faith, and more. In a sense, *tzedakah* is Judaism's Life-force, the mode of behavior that enlivens both giver and recipient, energizing, sometimes rejuvenating, revivifying—bringing to life those who may have been downtrodden, defeated, weary to their bones and souls. So many words, so much of the human being and the raw basics of what it is to be alive are associated with *tzedakah*.

Danny Siegel
Gym Shoes and Irises, Book Two

Our sages of blessed memory said: The quality of generosity depends on habit, for you cannot be considered generous unless you give of your own free will at all times, at all hours, according to your ability. Someone who gives a thousand gold pieces to a worthy person at one time is not as generous as one who on a thousand different occasions gives one gold piece each to a thousand worthy causes. This is because the person who gives a thousand gold pieces at once is acting on a sudden impulse and afterwards no longer has any desire to be generous.

Orot Tzaddikim

Rabbi Judah used to say: Ten strong things have been created in the world. The rock of the mountain is hard, but iron cleaves it. Iron is hard, but fire softens it. Fire is powerful, but water quenches it. Water is heavy, but clouds bear it. Clouds are thick, but wind scatters them. Wind is strong, but a body resists it. The body is strong, but fear crushes it. Fear is powerful, but wine banishes it. Wine is strong, but sleep works it off. Death is stronger than all, but *tzedakah* delivers from death, as it is written, "*Tzedakah* delivers from death" (Proverbs 10:2).

Babylonian Talmud, Baba Batra 10a

CHAPTER 15

Breaking Sacred Trusts Through Adultery/Making Covenants

B'gidah/Brit

The circle we have built together has unraveled.

Our covenant is broken, our souls are not bound up with each other.

The sounds of thunder and lightning, the sound of the shofar at the Sinai where we once stood together no longer echo in our ears.

We turn to you, Adonai, who stood with us then, to stand with us now, as we move out of the circle we drew together.

We ask you to stand with us now as we undo our covenant of marriage, acknowledging with great pain and sadness that through it we are no longer your partners in the process of tikkun olam.

Rather than add to the splintering of our own souls and rather than continue to let this marriage distance each of us from you, we unbind ourselves from the obligations of this marriage and with it, a part of each of us will be unraveled.

Contemporary Divorce Document
prepared by Rachel T. Sabath

This bride and groom enter into the obligations of marriage. They have declared to each other:

> *"Be consecrated unto me according to the laws of Moses and Israel. I will love, honor, and cherish you; I will protect and support you, and I will faithfully care for your needs. I pledge my love and devotion, and I take upon myself the fulfillment of the responsibilities of this covenant of marriage."*

from the Ketubah

Of all our relationships with others, there is none more concretely symbolized and documented, and, sadly, more often violated in our time, than the covenant between the two partners in a marriage. Everything in Jewish culture seeks to affirm this covenant, which traditionally is described as akin to the covenant of the entire people of Israel with God. Not surprisingly, in view of the intensity of the connection between the two parties, the Bible often compares the covenant with God to a marriage; and violations of the covenantal relationship—instances when the Jewish people were unfaithful to their divine "spouse"—bring the gravest of punishments: exile. (Take a look at Hosea 2:16 ff.)

While the covenant of marriage is usually entered with the expectation that it will last a lifetime, circumstances often change, especially when one spouse is not loyal to the other. This is a subject about which people don't like to talk. It's more than a "I don't want to judge my neighbor until I have stood in his/her shoes" attitude. We no longer even use the term "adultery" very often. Instead, we refer to infidelity to a spouse as an extramarital relationship, an affair, a fling.

Call it what you will, when one partner to an intimate relationship betrays the covenant made with the other, whether as part of a marital relationship or in a committed relationship between two persons without the benefit of marriage, a sacred trust has been broken. This is exactly what the Author of the Ten Commandments had in mind when writing, "Thou shalt not commit adultery."

The analogy between interhuman covenants and Israel's covenant with God permeates Judaism. What we declare to our Most Significant Other, "I will betroth you to me forever; and I will betroth you to me in righteousness and in judgment, and in loyal love, and in mercy, and I will betroth you to me in faithfulness" (Hosea 2:21), we also declare to our earthly significant others in marriage and in other seriously committed relationships.

This means that something of our relationship with God is interwoven into our relationships with other human beings (and that there is something of our relationships with others in our relationship with God). Consequently, when there is betrayal in a relationship with another human being, it is also a betrayal in the relationship with God. Both relationships are held up with high ideals, and as human beings we are capable of failing even in what is most important to us. This feeling of failure distances us from others and from God.

Sometimes betrayal is hard to measure. When one partner has a sexual encounter with someone outside the partnership, it's pretty obvious. But adultery does not always begin or end with a sexual encounter. Sometimes, sex is just a byproduct of adultery that grows out of the breaking of one person's trust and commitment to another. Sex is often totally unrelated to the breaking of a sacred trust. Often there is no sexual relationship between the individuals involved in the breaking of the covenant. That is one of the things that makes this *middah* so difficult. The *yetzer hara* drives us into more unsavory places than just our neighbor's bedroom.

Maintaining a relationship over a long time can be excruciatingly demanding, as everyone who has ever been in a relationship with another person will admit. Our lives are indeed filled with struggles of various kinds. At every turn, there is something ready to yank us off the path to becoming the person we want to become. There are temptations and betrayals of all kinds: emotional, intellectual, material. And yet betraying a commitment in order to satisfy an appetite is rarely satisfying, however insatiable the desire may seem.

Again the prophet Hosea speaks knowingly about what we have in mind: "For they will eat, but they will not have enough" (4:10). Those who give in to temptation often find themselves less satisfied than before. Pulled off track, we get lost—in exile from "an other." That's when the road leads us into someone else's arms.

But we can also be pulled back on track. Relationships may falter. They may fail, but they can also be reestablished and rebuilt. According to the midrash, many worlds were destroyed before the current one was created. God failed and tried again. So can we; failing in one relationship does not mean that we have lost the ability to enter and succeed in another.

Being in a sacred relationship with another person involves responsibility and commitment, neither of which can be maintained when the relationship is constantly threatened. Living in a binding covenant with another human being demands constant reaffirmation to keep the ties alive. The spiral winds both upward and downward, depending on how hard we work at it, and how much we nourish the relationship.

Recently a couple told Rachel the story of the adultery that had torn their relationship from its foundations. "We had stopped communicating," said one partner. "We had never really learned how to communicate in the first place," said the other. In retrospect, the two individuals described in great detail what they might have done to protect their covenant. Both agreed that they had not realized what a constant effort was needed to maintain a strong relationship and thus it was easy for them to see an "affair" as a natural symptom of a weakening bond. "I was like a wandering but persistent vine, looking for a place to cling and attach myself. I needed to direct that impulse, those desires, though to the garden in which I was planted and which I wanted to make beautiful."

These thoughts of regret with faith in human connectedness exemplify the natural but necessarily directed desires of the human personality. We want to cling to another person, making it possible for ourselves and the other to bloom, but there are necessarily times when a relationship comes to an end. When an interpersonal covenant once thought to be binding is terminated, this should be done in a manner that takes cognizance of the sacral character it once possessed and of the ritual with which it was initiated. The capacity to conclude a covenant is no less important than the ability to enter into one.

A covenant, the most sacred relational agreement between two persons, is powerful only when both partners feel that its presence is vital and its absence would be shattering. Normally we tend to play down the impact of losing a relationship and instead emphasize being in one, but there is something to be said for being afraid to lose a committed "other." There is something to be said for the power of the fear of losing what is most precious and close to the heart.

If the splintering of the soul that would occur were the covenant violated would be insufferable, the partners may seek to avoid this outcome at all costs, and will do everything possible to maintain and repair the relationship. Yet while such efforts sometimes succeed, at other times, in spite of everything, no repair is possible.

When Israel violated its covenant with God, the consequences were immediate and grave. When a marital covenant is violated, the consequences may not appear at once, but they will come inexorably and perniciously. Anyone who has ever felt the pain of betrayal knows that the violation of a relationship by a lover cuts deeply and has a powerful effect. Even when there are no tangible consequences, a broken covenant between two loved ones leaves scars everywhere. A famous philosopher once said that sin is ultimately what separates us. When we damage a sacred commitment, we are cut apart from a significant other, and ultimately from ourselves.

Knowing, Being, Doing

Reread your covenant of marriage. With your partner, decide what you will do today to affirm your commitment to each another. Write a new covenant, a renewal of the first one, taking into account how far you have come together. Acknowledge the struggles you now face and how you will confront them together by offering strength to one another.

If you are not married, write out a covenant you hope one day to uphold. If you have been married and are now divorced, write out a document of "release" that frees your former spouse from all roles in your life and frees you from all roles in his/her life. Permit yourself (and your former partner) to let go—and then to move on.

More On Breaking Sacred Trusts Through Adultery/Making Covenants

"That you do not follow your heart . . . in your lustful urge" (Numbers 15:39). Rabbi Judah the Patriarch said, "This verse teaches that you should not drink from one goblet while thinking about another."

Babylonian Talmud, Nedarim 20b

Resh Lakish said: "Don't think that you are an adulterer only if you actually commit the act with your body. Even if you do it only with your eyes you are, for it is said, 'The eyes also of the adulterer' (Job 24:15)."

Leviticus Rabbah 23:12

A story that accounts for the fall of Jerusalem and the destruction of the Second Temple: A certain man—a carpenter's apprentice—conceived a desire for his master's wife. There came a time when his master needed to borrow some money. The apprentice said, "Send your wife to me, and I will give her the money." The master sent his wife to the apprentice, and she stayed with him for three days. Finally, the master went to the apprentice's home and asked, "Where is my wife whom I sent to you?" The apprentice replied, "I sent her away at once, but I heard that on her way back some young men had their way with her." "What shall I do?" the master asked. "If you want my advice," the apprentice replied, "divorce her." But the master said, "But she has a large marriage settlement [payable in the event of a divorce]." The apprentice replied, "I'll lend you the money to pay her settlement." So the master divorced his wife, and the apprentice immediately married her. When the loan came due, the master was unable to pay it and so the apprentice said to him: "Come, work off your debt with me." Then the apprentice and his new wife would sit eating and drinking while the master waited on them, tears flowing from his eyes and dropping into their cups. From that hour, the doom [of Jerusalem] was sealed.

Babylonian Talmud, Gittin 58a

Rabbi Akiva taught, "If a husband and wife are worthy, the Divine Presence dwells in their midst. If they are not worthy, a fire consumes them."

Babylonian Talmud, Sotah 17a

Have mercy upon me, O God, as it befits Your faithfulness;
In keeping with Your abundant compassion, blot out my transgressions.
Wash me thoroughly of my iniquity, and purify me of my sin,
For I recognize my transgression and am ever conscious of my sin.
Purge me with hyssop till I am pure,
Wash me till I am whiter than snow. . . .
Fashion a pure heart for me, O God,
Create in me a steadfast spirit.
Do not cast me out of Your presence,
Or take Your holy spirit from me.
Let me again rejoice in Your help,
Let a vigorous spirit sustain me.
Let me teach transgressors Your ways
The sinners may return to You.

Psalm 51:3–5, 9, 12–15
said to have been written by King David
after he recognized the sin
of his adultery with Bathsheva

CHAPTER 16

Senseless Hatred/Committing to Love

Sinah/Ahavah

Some people make vows out of hatred of their neighbor,
swearing, for example, that they will not let this or
that person sit at the same table with them or come
under the same roof. Such people should seek the
mercy of God so that they may find some cure for the
diseases of their soul.

Philo of Alexandria

What has the Holy One been doing since creation?
According to one tradition, God has been busy making
matches, bringing together the daughter of so-and-so
with the son of so-and-so. On hearing this, a woman
once said: "If that is all God does, I can do the same
thing! In no time at all I can match them up." Rabbi
Yose said to her: "Matchmaking may be a trivial thing
in your eyes, but for the Holy One, it is as awesome an
act as splitting the Red Sea."

When Rabbi Yose left, what did the woman do? She
took a thousand young men and a thousand young
women, lined them up in rows facing each other, and
said, "This man will marry this woman, and this
woman shall be married to this man." In this way, she
matched them all up in a single night.

In the morning, when she returned, she saw one

*woman with a bloody head, another with bruises and
her hair disheveled, one man with his eyes knocked
out, one with his shoulder dislocated, and another
with his leg broken.*

*The woman asked: "What happened?" One of the
men replied, "I don't want that woman"; one of the
women replied, "I don't want that man."*

*The woman promptly sent for Rabbi Yose. "Great
teacher," she said, "your Torah is excellent and worthy
of praise. Everything you said is exactly so."*

Genesis Rabbah 68:4, Leviticus Rabbah 8:1,
Numbers Rabbah 3:6

One might think that Judaism would provide us with guidance on how to find our life's partner. And in a sense, it does. When we develop a moral approach to living, then we have a greater potential to build strong, abiding relationships with others.

In the Song of Songs we read about the erotic love of a man and a woman. The imagery is vivid and passionate, albeit through the prism of an ancient writer's view on the world of love. The rabbis understood this story as a metaphor for the loving relationship between humankind and God. For the rabbis, one relationship reflects the other. As we learn to love another person, we learn to love God. And as our love for another person being grows and matures, so does our love for God.

Building and nourishing a loving relationship is often difficult. By awakening our feeling of love for others, we awaken the love we have for God, which might otherwise remain hidden deep within our soul. The Baal Shem Tov, the founder of Chasidism, said, "When you fall in love with an earthly pleasure, consider that the power of love was given to you for the purpose of loving God, not for loving unworthy things. You will find it easy to serve God with the love awakened in your heart. Thus we read in the Song of Songs, 'How fair and how pleasant you are, O love, for delights!'

(7:7). Without the true feeling of love, stimulated by pleasure, it is difficult to feel true love for God" (*Midrash Ribesh Tov*).

In a similar vein, Rabbi Levi Yitzchak of Berditchev observed that you can determine whether someone really loves God by seeing whether he or she loves other people. Our attitude toward others, especially toward those we love or hope to develop a loving relationship with, says something about how we feel about God. Just as being angry at others often means that we are angry at God, loving others often indicates the intensity of our love for God.

Likewise, just as it is difficult to establish a family and become a parent when you have not resolved your feelings about your own parents and family, a failure to explore your relationship with God, the Ultimate Parent, can make it difficult to parent and really love a child. Rabbi Lawrence Kushner comments that we spend our lives trying to separate from our parents and remain close to our children. The paradox, of course, is that we are children even as we are parents. We are struggling with our own parents, or our memories of them, and at the very same time we are the parents of children who are struggling with us.

Yet there is no way to distinguish between loving others, loving God, and finally—or perhaps initially—loving ourselves. So we must simultaneously turn in three directions: toward ourselves, toward others, and toward God. Some days we can do this three-pointed turn with simple grace. Other times it is more complicated. Often we find ourselves tripping over our tongues and our feet, stumbling toward something that propels and inspires us inexplicably.

Unless we maintain this triune focus, and succeed in probing the mysteries of all three relationships—with self, others, and God—two of them, at least, will falter. In a dizzying state from perpetually moving in so many directions, it is tempting to accept a blurry status quo. Only when each relationship is in focus can it become a source of increasing ability to show love: one for the other.

Knowing, Being, Doing
Try using one lens on love to improve your vision of another. As you consider your love for God, use it as a prism to love your

spouse, your partner, your child, your neighbor, or your friend. Then try it the other way. Use your love for someone else as a prism to visualize and then express your love for God. Ask for caring blessings to surround them and ask God to protect and bless those you love. Remember to ask for love for yourself too, so that you become a vehicle for more love.

More On Senseless Hatred/Committing To Love

Rabbi Moses Leib of Sassov taught, "To know the needs of others and bear the burden of their sorrow, that is true love."

We are loved by an unending love.
We are embraced by arms that find us
even when we are hidden from ourselves.

We are touched by fingers that soothe us
even when we are too proud for soothing.
We are counseled by voices that guide us
even when we are too embittered to hear.
We are loved by an unending love.

We are supported by hands that uplift us
even in the midst of a fall.
We are urged on by eyes that meet us
even when we are too weak for meeting.
We are loved by an unending love.

Embraced, touched, soothed, counseled . . .
ours are the arms, the fingers, the voices;
ours are the hands, the eyes, the smiles;
We are loved by an unending love.

Rabbi Rami M. Shapiro

The Baal Shem Tov was asked, "How are we to serve God if it is true, as you teach, that fasting and self-chastisement are sinful?" He replied, "The main thing is to encompass yourself in love of God, love of Israel, and love of Torah. You will attain this by eating enough to preserve your health and making use of your strength to battle against the evil inclination."

Set me as a seal upon your heart, as a seal upon your arm; for love is as strong as death, and passion as unquenchable. Its flashes are flashes of fire, a divine flame. Many waters cannot quench love, neither can floods drown it. If you were to offer everything you owned for love, you would be utterly scorned.

Song of Songs 8:6–7

Before beginning to pray in the synagogue . . . take upon yourself the precept "and you shall love your neighbor as yourself" (Leviticus 19:18). And concentrate on loving every member of the house of Israel as you love yourself. If you do this, your prayers will ascend, bound up with the prayers of Israel. By this means, your soul will be able to rise above and effect *tikkun*.

And especially when it comes to the love of the colleagues with whom you study Torah, each and every one of you must bind yourself to the others, as if your study group were a body and each of you one of its limbs. This is particularly important when you have the knowledge and mystical insight to understand and apprehend a friend's soul. And if one of you should be in distress, all of you must take it upon yourselves to share in the trouble, whether it is an illness or a problem with children, God forbid. And you must all pray on the other's behalf. Likewise, in all your prayers and petitions, be mindful of your fellows.

Isaac Luria

What mode of loving God is appropriate? Is it loving God with a love so extraordinarily powerful that your soul becomes tied to the love of God so that you pine for it unceasingly? It should be as if you were lovesick, unable to get the person you love out of your mind, pining for that person all the time when you eat or drink. Even more than this should be the love of God in the hearts of those who love God and yearn constantly for God, as God instructed us, "with all your heart and with all soul" (Deuteronomy 6:5).

Moses Maimonides
Mishneh Torah, Hilchot Teshuvah 10:3

CHAPTER 17

Failing a Companion/Cleaving to a Friend
Remiah/Dibbuk Chaverim

There are many kinds of thieves: those who steal the hearts of people, those who invite their neighbors to be their guests when in their hearts they do not really mean it, those who offer gifts to their neighbors knowing that they will not be accepted.

Mekhilta de Rabbi Ishmael, Nezikin 13

When Rabbi Eleazar concluded his Tefillah, he would add: "May it be Your will, Adonai our God, that in our lot there dwell love and congeniality, peace and friendship. May You make our lands abundant in disciples. To the very end of our lives, may You endow us with hope and expectation. May You set our portion in Paradise. May You sustain us in Your world with a good friend and a good impulse.

Babylonian Talmud, Berachot 17a

Sigmund Freud said that our central psychological need is to love and to work. It seems like common sense. We all have our life's work to do. Sometimes it forms the nexus for a vocation or career; sometimes it is a voluntary activity or even something we do with neighborhood children, like coaching Little League or being a Brownie Leader.

Through love we establish and nurture relationships with others. Relationships take many forms, and the list of potential partners is endless: parent and child, teacher and student, coworkers, spouses, lovers, neighbors. All relationships, even the strongest, are marked by challenges.

Friendship is one of the most common interpersonal relationships. It takes a variety of structures and poses many challenges, depending on the nature and character of one's friendship partner.Regardless of the specific situation, friendship has the potential to become a source of great meaning in our lives.

Whether we are sorrowful or joyful, we like to share our experiences with others. It is part of what makes us human. Sharing makes friendships stronger. Shared experiences, time together, in-depth conversations, exchanges of hopes and fears, and a sense of trust—all of these activities have the potential to build friendships between individuals.

As friendship grow in intensity, they ascend to high levels. New friends share excitement about the future. Old friends share a history together which is marked by a commitment to celebration and sorrow.

Ben Sirach summarized it this way: "A faithful friend is a powerful defense. One who has found such a friend has found a treasure" (Ecclesiasticus 6:14).

Rabbi Shlomo Carlebach taught us a great deal about friendship. For him, a friend was much more than an acquaintance. Rabbi Carlebach defined an acquaintance as someone who may be prepared to do something you ask, but only when asked, and only what is specifically asked. A friend, on the other hand, knows your needs—often before you are aware of them or articulate them. It isn't necessary to ask a friend to do something for you; he or she will already have done it, even before you are able to articulate the need for yourself.

Central to friendship is intimate knowledge of the other person. Friendship is perhaps the oldest form of relationship between two human beings. In Genesis, Eve becomes Adam's friend—to engage him, help him, and oppose him, as an *ezer k'negdo*—before she becomes a lover or a partner in procreation.

Like Adam and Eve, all human beings seek out someone to mitigate their sense of loneliness, alienation, and despair. Thus, Adam and Eve formed the first friendship in the most profound sense of the word. The first relationship in the world was also the first friendship.

But friendship also comes in forms that differ from the one established by Adam and Eve. The rabbis stressed the kind of friendship that emerges from studying or learning Torah together. Many of us are familiar with the bonding that occurs when people go on camping trips together or engage in some joint project. Encountering the intricacies of Torah together provides a different kind of adventure.

The legends of our sacred tradition have a great deal to say about the kind of friendship that develops when individuals join together to grapple with words of Torah. At its highest level, this relationship was called *dibbuk chaverim,* a cleaving between friends that transcends all other levels of friendship. It describes a merging of minds and souls and the deepest level of understanding. This status is achieved only by the most ideal friendships.

The idea of *dibbuk chaverim*, or clinging to another person (as opposed to clinging to God, *devekut*), is rooted in the friendship between Adam and Eve. "And when a man leaves the house of his father and mother . . . and clings to her" (Genesis 2:24). The combination of the ideas of friendship and cleaving unto another into an independent idea is what makes this concept so important.

In the midrash, *dibbuk chaverim* is one of the many attributes which leads to inner peace and personal fulfillment, uniquely combining a sense of community, intense intellectual engagement, and commitment to the partner with whom we study and move through the greatest challenges. When two individuals who learn together respect each other's thoughts and insights, their relationship can lead to the greatest goal.

Knowing, Being, Doing

Are your most important friendships at the level of *dibbuk chaverim*? Is your commitment to your friend so unswerving that you would struggle with him/her over the meaning of the events and ideas that shape your lives? What is different about a friendship that has developed out of a discussion of conflicting ideas? After thinking about these questions, imagine yourself with your closest friend or confidant (a study partner if you already have one). What would you say to your friend that might describe the beauty of your friendship? In what ways has your friendship led to peace in each of your lives and in the broader community? Now imagine all of the friends with whom you have struggled over ideas throughout your life. Envision all of them before you, surrounding you, and feel them cleaving, clinging to you, waiting to move with you through the next stage in life. Emboldened by their friendship and support, take the next step forward.

More on Cheating a Neighbor/Cleaving to a Friend

What is the good path to which one should adhere? Rabbi Joshua said, "To be a morally good companion." Rabbi Yose said, "To be a good neighbor." What is the evil path that one should shun? Rabbi Joshua said, "Being a bad companion and a false friend." Rabbi Yose said, "Being a bad neighbor."

Pirke Avot 2: 13–14

The person who asks God's mercy for a friend while in need of the same thing will be answered first, for it is said, "Adonai changed the fortune of Job when he prayed for a friend" (Job 42:10).

Babylonian Talmud, Baba Kamma 92a

We become great through friendship and learning together, through studying Torah, and finding compromises.

adapted from Tanna d'Bei Eliyahu Zuta 17

When you make a friend, begin by testing him and be in no hurry to trust him.

Some friends are loyal when it suits them but desert you in time of trouble.

Some friends turn into enemies and shame you by making your quarrels public.

Another sits at your table but is nowhere to be found in time of trouble; when you are prosperous, he will be with your second self and make use of your servants,

but if you come down in the world, he will turn against you and you will not see him again.

Hold your enemies at a distance and keep a wary eye on your friends.

A faithful friend is a secure shelter; whoever finds one has found a treasure.

A faithful friend is beyond praise; his worth is more than money can buy. . . .

Do not desert an old friend; a new one is not worth as much.

Ben Sirach 6:7–15, 9:10

And how can you love your friend with a perfect heart? By always remembering your friend for good, always thinking of your friend in honorable circumstances, always speaking good of your friend, averting your eyes from your friend's failings and offenses, reproving privately when your friend acts improperly, rejoicing in memories of your friend, finding your friend's words pleasant and not burdensome, being solicitous of your friend's love, lovingly lowering yourself before your friend and humbling your heart in friendly service, seeking always through your deeds to ingratiate yourself with your friend, loving those who love your friend and hating those who hate your friend, and guiding your friend in the way of Torah and mitzvot. Anyone who does this with a certainty loves his friend with a perfect love.

Sefer Ma'alot Ha-Middot

Moving Toward God

CHAPTER 18

Living Without Order/Establishing a Prayerful Posture
Hefkerut/Tefillah

It is not you alone, or we, or those others who pray; all things pray, all things pour forth their souls. The heavens pray, the earth prays, every creature and every living thing prays. In all life, there is longing. Creation is itself but a longing, a kind of prayer to the Almighty. What are the clouds, the rising and the setting of the sun, the soft radiance of the moon, and the gentleness of the night? What are the flashes of the human mind and the storms of the human heart? They are all prayers—the outpouring of boundless longing for God.

Micha Yosef Berdichevski
Tefillah Shebalev

Some readers may wonder why we have included prayer as one of the moral attributes. It is not so much prayer itself as the attitude toward prayer, the ability and desire to pray, that is a *middah*, because it is the inclination to pray, and not necessarily any particular prayer, that has inherent moral potential.

The *middah* of maintaining a prayerful posture goes far beyond the act of praying. It helps us to order our lives. It is a state of mind which reflects how we approach prayer, and how our approach to prayer affects the way we perceive the world and those around us. It also reflects how we perceive ourselves in relation to God. When we combine a prayerful posture with the requisite constancy of nurture and development, then prayer, and our perspective on it, will inform everything we do and everything we are and will become.

Life is filled with opportunities for prayer, but we are often not mindful of them. Traditionally Jews were required to recite a blessing on waking, on eating, on using the toilet, on all sorts of occasions. In fact, the rabbis held that reciting a minimum of one hundred blessings a day was necessary simply to celebrate experiencing the world and being mindful of the miracle of being alive.

Tradition also holds that there are three times a day when fixed, formal prayer is appropriate, morning (*shacharit*), afternoon (*min-*

cha), and evening (*maariv*), and these were the times of the three daily services in the synagogue. In addition, there are unlimited opportunities throughout the day for the outpouring of the heart in prayer, from the time we arise in the morning (and recite Modeh Ani in gratitude for having been granted another day of life) until the time we go to sleep at night (after reciting Shema al Ha-Mitah).

Each of these occasions presents us with an additional opportunity to continue our ongoing dialogue with God. If we don't seize the opportunities to pray provided by our normal routines, we may find ourselves unable to initiate the conversation when a deep-felt need to speak to the Divine arises, as often happens to those who wait for the Holy Days before opening up to God.

The rabbis of the Talmud put it this way: "We have been taught 'To love Adonai your God and to serve God with all your heart' (Deuteronomy 11:13). What service is 'with the heart'? Certainly, the service of the heart is prayer" (Babylonian Talmud, Ta'anit 2a; *Shulchan Aruch* 523:157).

For some people, the notion of suddenly establishing a prayerful posture may feel uncomfortable or, at best, jarring. Praying will seem strange at first, and comfort will be hard-won. For others, prayer will quickly bring a longed-for sense of balance and meaning.

Learning to feel at ease while praying is not unlike learning anything new. All new activities take some measure of practice and concentration, and also necessitate the development of the requisite skills and a personal commitment to incorporate the new activity into the pattern of one's life. That is why we begin with the attitude toward prayer. If you can develop the necessary mind-set—the motivation, desire, need, to pray—it will lead you to begin, even if only with hesitant, frightened steps.

Only after we change our thinking about prayer can we begin to pray meaningfully. Just as a jogger's initial struggle to complete a half-mile run eventually becomes the intense thrill of finishing a ten-mile race, entering into prayer with one simple blessing will quickly lead to the thrill of praying a full service and imagining the ecstasy of communion with God, the merging of one's sense of self with the Divine Other.

Establishing a prayerful posture in one's life begins the first morning you open up a prayer book or enter a synagogue filled with early-morning strangers. If you continue steadily on this path, even if you are sometimes discouraged and uncomfortable, prayer will eventually begin to feel familiar and offer its unique kind of solace. Time and effort will be needed before you begin to feel any sense of mastery; even then, as in a challenging program of exercise, a level of uneasiness will remain—the level of struggle to maintain one's faith in God and belief in self.

There may be a constant wrestling with yourself. Unlike physical exercise, whose primary purpose is the building of muscles and toning of body, the ultimate focus in prayer is to connect oneself to God. Routine exercise makes the process of strengthening our bodies somewhat easier, but as we grow to feel a closeness with the Holy One of Being, our struggles may seem greater.

Those who pray regularly develop a certain outlook on the world. The stance of prayer is the stance of a human being standing before God and directing his or her heart toward Jerusalem, the spiritual core of the world and its holiest place, where the Temple once stood. It is, in fact, what we may call a psycho-spiritual posture.

We maintain this posture by getting in tune with the Jewish ritual calendar, anchored by our prayers, which reflect the history of our people's relationship with God. According to Rabbi David Teutsch, "The rhythms of ritual provide a powerful sense of the holy dimension in each day, week, month and year. The words of the *siddur* and the actions that accompany them create a ritual structure that enables us to sense the dimension of the holy. That ability becomes ours when we take on the aspirations, make commitments of time and energy, and discipline ourselves for the task."

Just as one centers oneself to develop endurance to become a long-distance runner, establishing a prayerful posture also requires a kind of centering, a focus of the entire self toward a single goal: communication with God. It matters not whether the prayer comes through the words of the prayer book or the words of one's heart.

Developing a prayerful posture requires participation in the experience of prayer. You may begin by watching others pray and intellectualizing the prayer experience, but eventually you have to do it on your own. Rabbi Pinchas of Koretz said that thinking you can learn to pray by watching others do it is as foolish as thinking you can learn to walk a tightrope by watching someone else. Watch all you want, but eventually you have to go out on your own. If you don't extend your foot and take that difficult first step, you will surely fall into the abyss. So too you must find your own way to stand before God and commune with the Creator.

Ultimately, each of us must find our own balance in prayer in order to walk across our own spiritual tightrope. This is the only way to cross over whatever separates us from God. Developing a prayerful posture, then, means developing a sense of spiritual balance, a real sense of grace, in prayer. The more balanced you become, the more focused, the more fluent and familiar you become with prayer, the more it will flow from your mouth and into your heart—and directly to God. It will enable you to walk across the tightrope; it will give voice to the yearning of your soul.

Simply put, a prayerful posture means toning your body, mind, and heart to be strong enough to allow God into your life. "Where is God?" asked the students of Menachem Mendl of Kotzk, a rather enigmatic Chasidic teacher. Came his profoundly simple reply, "Wherever we let God in."

Knowing, Being, Doing

Meditation offers a prelude to prayer. Meditation helps to ready us for prayer. It helps us focus our thoughts and direct our hearts toward God. Try using the last verse of Psalm 150, which talks about the instruments that can be used to praise God, as a *kavannah*, a Jewish mantra for prayer: *Kol haneshamah t'hallel Yah* "Let every living soul praise God with breath." The goal is not to see how fast you can say these words; repeat them slowly, softly, over and over until they cannot be distinguished from one another, until you are no longer conscious of what you are saying, or even that you are saying anything. *Kol haneshamah t'hallel Yah. Kol haneshamah t'hallel Yah. Kol haneshamah t'hallel Yah.* Let the words take you into the inner precincts of your soul. Only there can you begin your prayer to God.

More on Living Without Order/ Establishing a Prayerful Posture

To want to pray, but only alone and only for oneself, seems to make too much of self and too little of God. Judaism commands communal prayer because God cares for all as God cares for each one, because, while God is the God of each private individual, God is the God of all individuals as well. The single self is indispensable. Without any one, humankind is incomplete. So too, without all other selves, equally precious to God, the single self looses its context and hence its final significance. Humans cannot find themselves only in others, but humans also cannot find themselves without them. If prayer is supposed to open the human to the truth of one's existence, it must begin with self, but it must reach out to all humankind.

adapted from Rabbi Eugene B. Borowitz

Prayer is a brazen act. For it is brazen to stand and address God, the Holy Blessed One. One way or another, we all have some awareness of the greatness of the Creator. How then can we stand in prayer before God? For prayer is a wonder, its task is chiefly to assault, and despoil, the heavenly order. . . . Human beings come to despoil the order and do marvels. Therefore, you must be shameless in prayer.

Nachman of Bratzlav
Likutey Etzot Ha-Shem

Studying or praying with reverence and love binds us in thought to the Creator, the Holy Blessed One. We see and hear nothing except the divine vitality that permeates all things. For everything is from God, blessed be God's name; only it is clothed, as it were, in various garments. Motives of self and worldly desire will not enter your mind if you focus your thoughts on the vitality of the Creator and the spiritual delight that inheres in all things.

Dov Baer, the Maggid of Mezritch
Esser Orot

In prayer, you gather the strength of dedication for life, allowing this life to become the fulfillment of the divine will, the furthering of the divine purpose—a contribution to the success of the purpose that God has set for humanity and Israel. Thus the flower of all prayer is the resolution which infuses the whole person and unites all your powers to be a servant of God in life.

Joseph Albo
Sefer Ha-Ikkarim

Prayer means a full consciousness of God's presence and of our relation with God. It is a more intimate being with God, a talking with God, the offering of our love, our gratitude, our adoration. In prayer humans are putting themselves, or trying to put themselves, on the side of God. It is a declaration of loyalty to God, and loyalty to God implies a readiness to make God's aim our aim. God's aim is the increase of spiritual and moral goodness in the world, to lead the universe toward perfection. God's laws are in their working organized toward this end. The one who is loyal to God must organize his or her life to be within the sphere of the workings of these laws. True prayer is the opening of our hearts Godward, and the answer is a flow of light and influence from God. True prayer is the desire to put ourselves into line with God's providence, the answer is an increased working of that providence in and through our lives. True prayer is a search for God, the answer is finding God.

adapted from Rabbi Israel Mattuck

CHAPTER 19

Thanklessness/Showing Gratitude
Kefiut Tovah/Hoda'ah

In explaining Psalm 145, which expresses gratitude to God, Rabbi Samson Raphael Hirsch taught that it is essentially the soul that praises God. Of all the facets of the human being, he argued, the soul is best qualified to recognize God, because it responds to the revelation of divine greatness apparent in God's mighty acts. And the soul is also most able to proclaim the demonstration of divine power for all to hear, for it is aware that it is the "invisible personality" that is the basic cause of all the effects that emanate from it. And by virtue of its awareness of its own nature, the soul is capable of attributing all the phenomena of nature and events of history to the One God who is the one "invisible personality" from which all things flow.

Waking up in the morning can seem like the most common and uncelebrated part of the day. For some of us, it is also the most difficult part of the day. Struggling to get out of bed, mustering the strength to face the challenges that lie ahead, most of us are not usually struck with the impulse to thank God. There are too many other things clouding our minds: things we have to do at work or school or around the house, errands to run, shopping to do. Gratitude for another day of life is overshadowed by fatigue, stress, the blaring sound of the alarm, a crying baby, or just the commonplace calls of nature in the morning.

Too often, at that early hour, we seem unaware of the gift of life, much less of God's existence, especially before the first cup of a warming but decaffeinated coffee. Then, browsing through the morning paper, we begin to feel the force of the day picking up in us, and perhaps, from time to time, are struck by the beauty of the dawn or the mystery of life's cyclical pattern.

The chorus of morning repeats itself in the Bible, where in the first few paragraphs we read over and over: "And there was evening and there was morning, a first . . . second . . . third . . . fourth . . . fifth . . . sixth day." The wonder of the biblical story of the first week of creation climaxes with the creation of Adam and Eve. The conclusion is the completion of creation, and God's cosmic pause: Shabbat.

We too take pauses. We call them Sabbaths. Sometimes, when we pause, we are overcome by a sense of wonder and gratitude for the good things, the special people and events which have helped shape our lives.

More intense moments of gratitude often accompany milestone events like celebrations, birthdays, sickness and recovery, birth and death. It's easy to see why large moments of this kind might lead us to pause and offer thanks to something or someone greater than ourselves. The birth of a child brings the parents a joy like none other in life. Recovery from a serious illness induces a sense of thankfulness for the body's power to heal. Even the death of a loved one, which always comes too soon regardless of the loved one's age, can prompt a kind of thankfulness for the moments we shared. It is no wonder that these larger moments of life move us to want to offer thanks.

But where is the gratitude for our daily lives, the routine activities that comprise most of our waking hours? What reminds us of the miracle of morning as we awaken to a new day? Upon getting out of bed, with our feet just touching the floor, our tradition suggests that we immediately recite the prayer of gratitude: *Modeh/modah ani l'fanecha* "Here I stand grateful to You, God." These few simple words cultivate our sense of God's presence in the most basic of human activities, waking up after being asleep.

> I exist before You in gratitude.
> For it is You, the One who created me together with my mother and father,
> Who has continued to cause the breath of life to exist within me.
> Thank You for this compassion and mercy.
> I am grateful just to wake up in the morning and be alive.

The tradition of washing one's hands upon arising from sleep stresses the newness of each day and the transition from being alive unconsciously to being consciously alive. Many of our prayers, shaped by the Book of Psalms, verbalize a similar sense of wonder at the gift of life, praising God, who grants life, and who fills the world in which we live with wonder. Even while struggling with the challenges of daily life—something we all do—when we stop to ponder its intricacies and its small pleasures, we are often aroused to a sense of gratitude impossible to explain, much less to articulate in words.

Throughout history human beings have felt enormous gratitude and sought to express it in art, in music, in words, and in deed. While we are more than just the "people of the book," the greatest Jewish texts contain numerous words of thanksgiving offered to God. Many of them are attempts from different eras to describe our people's sense of gratitude to God for everything from the creation of the world to the creation of the human race; from the liberation from slavery in Egypt to the revelation of Torah at Mount Sinai.

Scattered throughout the countless words of prayer is one thought which demonstrates the response that emerges because we are rejoicing on that single day: "This is the day that God has made, let us rejoice and be happy " (Psalm 118:24). Reflecting the imagery utilized by the psalmist, these prayers assert that there should be a ringing out of voices, a burst of music from instruments, and a large gathering of all the nations of the world, all in order to praise God. The text voices a kind of frustration at the limitation of words to express gratitude:

> Were our mouths filled with song as the sea [is with water],
> And our tongue with the ringing praise as the roaring waves.
> Were our lips full of adoration as the wide expanse of heaven,
> And our eyes sparkling like the sun or the moon.
> Were our hands spread out in prayer as eagles' wings in the sky,
> And our feet as swift as the deer,
> We should still be unable to thank You enough, Adonai our God.
> Praised are You, O God to whom thanksgiving is due.
>
> *Babylonian Talmud, Berachot 59b*

Recognizing that our ability to articulate thanks is limited by the confined nature of words, one rabbi, writing about the Book of Leviticus, said that even in the time to come, after the world has been perfected and the Messiah has arrived, when all of our prayers will be unnecessary and will have ceased, we will continue to give voice to a prayer of thanksgiving (Leviticus Rabbah 9:7).

Knowing, Being, Doing

Choose a single moment that occurs every day—such as exercising, eating, or even taking a vitamin—and consider adding a ritual which will demonstrate your gratitude for it. Next time the moment occurs, stop and say aloud or in a soft whisper to yourself, "Thank you." And begin to develop a short *kavannah*, or sacred Jewish mantra, which includes gratitude for the gift of daily life. You may want to take a cue from Doug Cotler, a contemporary Jewish songwriter and singer; he likes to simply do it this way: "*Baruch atah Adonai* . . . Thank you God."

More On Thanklessness/Showing Gratitude

Dov Baer of Mezritch said: "We read in our siddur for Shabbat 'Though our mouths were filled with song as the sea . . . yet would we be unable to thank You. . . . Therefore, the limbs which you have given us. . . . They will thank You.' There seems to be a contradiction between these two statements. But it is clarified by the following parable: A king informed one of his generals that he wanted to have lunch with him in the general's home. The general was bewildered, because he did not have the proper dishes to serve food 'fit for a king.' Sensing the general's ambivalence, the king told him, 'My cooks will prepare the food in order to save you the trouble.' Likewise, God desires our praise, but we tremble at the thought that our mouths are unable to utter the proper words and that we lack the proper spirit. But then we remind ourselves that we have been created by God, and we sense that God will accept our words through the very vessels God has formed.

Ben-Zoma once saw a large crowd on the steps of the Temple Mount. He exclaimed: "Blessed is the One who has created all these people to serve the divinity." Ben-Zoma also customarily said: "What labors did Adam have to carry out before he obtained bread to eat? He plowed. He sowed. He reaped. He bound the sheaves, threshed the grain, winnowed the chaff, selected the ears, ground them, sifted the flour, kneaded the dough, and baked it. Only then was he able to eat. On the other hand, I get up and find that all these things have already been done for me. Similarly, how many labors did Adam have to carry out before he obtained a garment to wear? He had to shear the sheep, wash the wool, comb it, spin it, and weave it. Then did he have a garment to wear. All I have to do is get up and find that these things too have been done for me. All kinds of artisans have come to my home so that when I awake in the morning, I find these things ready for me.

Babylonian Talmud, Berachot 58a

Like jumping into a pool, saying a *beracha* shocks you into paying attention.

Like jumping into a pool, saying a *beracha* immerses you totally.

Like jumping into a pool, saying a *beracha* forces you to find a way (back) up.

Like jumping into a pool, saying a *beracha* can really wake you up.

Like drinking from a well, saying a *beracha* brings you something from The Source.

Like drinking from a well, saying a *beracha* refreshes and renews you.

Like drinking from a well, saying a *beracha* is something you need.

Like drinking from a well, saying a *beracha* is a reward.

Joel Lurie Grishaver
and his students

The Radziminer Rebbe, Rabbi Jacob Aryeh, said, "One who crosses the ocean and is rescued from a shipwreck gives thanks to God. Should we not thank God if we cross without a mishap? One who is cured of a dangerous illness offers praise to God. Should we not praise God when God grants us health and preserves us from illness?"

I will glorify you, my God, my Sovereign Ruler. I praise You throughout all time. Everyday do I praise You, exalting Your glory forever. I will praise Adonai all my life, sing to my God with all my being.

from the prayer book, adapted from the Psalms

CHAPTER 20

Giving in to Despair/Opening to Hope
Ye'ush/Tikvah

Rabbi Joshua ben Levi met the prophet Elijah standing at the entrance to the cave of Rabbi Simon bar Yochai. He asked him when the Messiah would come. Elijah replied, "Go and ask him yourself."

"Where shall I find him?" asked Rabbi Joshua.

"Outside the gates of Rome."

"And how shall I recognize him?" asked Rabbi Joshua.

Elijah responded, "He will be sitting among the poor people, covered with wounds. The others unbind all their wounds at once and then bind them up again. But he unbinds each of his wounds separately and then immediately rebinds it. He says to himself, 'If I am needed, I must be ready to go and not be late.'"

So Rabbi Joshua went to the gates of Rome and found him. "Peace be with you, my master and teacher."

He answered, "And peace be with you, son of Levi."

Rabbi Joshua continued, "When are you coming, master?" Thereupon he answered, "Today."

So Rabbi Joshua returned to Elijah and said, "He deceived me. He said he would come today, but he has not come."

But Elijah responded, "This is what he meant: 'Today—if you would hearken to God's voice' (Psalm 95:7)."

Babylonian Talmud, Sanhedrin 98a

The prophet Jeremiah describes God as the "hope of Israel" (Jeremiah 14:8, 17:13). Rabbi Eliezer took Jeremiah's words to mean that God will enable Israel to get to the place it is striving to reach (Midrash Tehillim 4:9). Our sacred literature often invokes the idea of trusting and hoping in God, as if to say that the idea of God—the idea that God can change reality—inherently inspires hope.

Whatever one's personal theology, hope (*tikvah*) is an intangible source of the strength necessary to persevere and struggle through nearly any ordeal. Yet hope cannot always be found when it is needed. It does not lie latent, ready to be employed whenever we seek to call it up.

No, hope must be developed and nurtured. Sometimes it emerges like a rushing stream, racing downard from the glaciers melting atop some faraway mountain range to provide water for those who thirst below. And sometimes hope is a isolated rivulet, barely dripping onto the human heart to save it from consuming itself in despair.

In the Bible, hope is referred to as an open gate (Hosea 2:17) and as the opposite of evil (Proverbs 11:7). Those who are most pitied and most lost, says the biblical author, are the ones whose hope has turned to despair. In Job 11:20, hope is described as a "turning over in the soul." It was Job's faith, Job's hope, which enabled him to survive his ordeal; it could not be beaten out of him regardless of what happened. The same is true of many who have survived terrible disasters. In our own struggles, hope can help us to move through personal crises and save us from despair

Hope is an attitude about the future, a perspective which influences how we perceive the world, others, and ourselves. In the face of the worst catastrophes, hope enables us to imagine ourselves as surviving; and in many instances, the very act of imagining our own survival is what gives us the fortitude that enables us to survive.

When the Temple was destroyed, the Jewish people were exiled from the land of Israel. The hope, kept alive over the generations, that someday Jews would return to Jerusalem and rebuild it is what enabled Jews and Judaism to survive over the next two thousand years.

Without hope, surely it would be impossible to change, to grow, to improve. Rabbi Mordecai Kaplan, the founder of Reconstructionism, taught that there are practical and political manifestations of a particularly Jewish kind of hope, what we might call Jewish optimism.

Throughout Jewish history, hope has manifested itself in political and national movements, exploding in a way that cannot be contained. Much of what we are taught by the Jewish tradition supports this idea even in the face of unspeakable evils like the Holocaust. Central to inextinguishable hope of this kind is the concept of *teshuvah*, or repentance: the belief that even the worst deeds can be forgiven, even the greatest traumas can be overcome. That regardless of how we may distance ourselves from others, from God, and from ourselves, there is always the possibility, always the hope, always the prayer that we can return.

The greatest of Jewish hopes, beyond the actualized hope of returning to Zion expressed in Hatikvah, the Israeli national anthem, is the hope for the coming of the Messiah or the Messianic Age. We get a glimpse of the messianic future on Shabbat. The twenty-five hours of the Sabbath help us to see what is possible. Most Jewish thinkers maintain that we have to work to bring the Messiah, joining with others in making the world a better place in which all humankind will be able to live peacefully. This is a never-dying hope that the world, regardless of its brokenness, can be repaired and redeemed. Our hope is a sacred optimism.

According to Charles Vernoff, "Hope as a Judaic spiritual attitude has its basis in the covenant relation between God and Israel." In this sense, we cannot sustain a relationship with God without hope. And without hope, our ongoing relationship with God is at risk. God teaches us hope by never letting us go, by forever maintaining the covenant with us, and by sustaining us with hope, regardless of how we fail in sacred human obligations. We can become more than we are now.

Knowing, Being, Doing

Prayer is a way of hope, a way to change the natural order. So begin each day with a prayer that reflects your hope for the day. If the words do not flow naturally from your heart to your lips, and you need help, use a prayer book, for the Siddur contains the collective hopes of the Jewish people throughout its history. After praying, make sure you do something to help move your prayer toward reality.

More on Giving In to Despair/Opening to Hope

You must never say, "We have come to journey's end."
When days are dark, and clouds upon our world descend,
Believe the dark will lift, and freedom will yet appear,
Our marching feet will tell the world that we are here.

From sunny lands of palms to lands bedecked with snow,
We came with all our grief, with all our people's woe.
Where our martyr's precious blood the tyrant drew,
Our hope will yet receive, our life we shall renew.

The dawn will break, our world will still be robed in light,
Our agony will pass and vanish as the night.
But if our hoped-for rescue should arrive too late,
This song will tell the world the meaning of our fate.

No poet's playful muse inspired my pen to write,
I wrote my song amidst the anguish of the night.
we sang it as we watched the flames engulf the world,
It is a banner of defiance we unfurled.

You must never say, "We have come to journey's end."
When days are dark, and clouds upon the world descend,
Believe the dark will lift, and freedom yet appear,
Our marching feet will tell the world that we are here.

The Partisans' Song

You will find: Every place where Israel was exiled, the Shechinah [God's Presence] dwelled with them. They were exiled to Egypt, the Shechinah was with them. They were exiled to Babylon, the Shechinah was with them. They were exiled to Elam, the Shechinah was with them. They were exiled to Rome, the Shechinah was with them. And when they return, the Shechinah, *keveyachol* [as it were], will be with them.

Mekhilta to Exodus 12:51

We are weak, and the task seems hopeless, until we remember that we are not alone. There is a grace that every dawn renews, a loveliness making every daybreak fresh. We will endure, we will prevail, we shall see the soul restored to joy, the hand returned to strength, the will regain its force. We shall walk with hope—we the children of God who crowded the heaven with stars, endowed the earth with glory, and filled our souls with wonder.

Rabbi Chaim Stern

As long as deep in the heart
The soul of a Jew yearns
And towards the East
An eye looks to Zion

Our hope is not yet lost
The hope of two thousand years
To be a free people in our land
The land of Zion and Jerusalem

Naphtali Herz Imber
from Hatikvah, Israel's national anthem

The distinctive mood of the Jewish religion is, of all things, hope. It is obviously not a simple trust that God will literally not suffer us to stumble. Egypt was our house of bondage for four centuries before it was the place of the Exodus. And before Auschwitz and Treblinka, there was Assyrian genocide, Roman savagery, Crusader zeal and Cossack brutality. Jewish hope is not to be disassociated from Jewish suffering. It is born in Jewish pain; that is why Jews have known how, religiously, to sigh. . . . But Jewish tragedy is not the whole of God's truth nor even the most important truth.

. . . What surprises, astonishes, moves, determines, the Jew is his [or her] realization, born of the experience of the Jewish people, that there is another, greater power moving through human events than [hu]man's brutality to [hu]man. The story of the survival of this improbable people is its chief testimony. The Jews have known not one but many Exoduses. All of them have been, if history has laws or repetitive patterns—miracles. Just by being here, then, the Jewish people is an evidence of hope. And when the Jewish people is faithful in practice to the God it knows has kept it alive, despite the mammoth historical forces arrayed against it, it is an active force for hope. . . .

Rabbi Eugene B. Borowitz

CHAPTER 21

Expressing Disbelief/Embracing Faith
Apikorsut/Emunah

Rabbi Judah ben Illai said, "God's parental care for Israel is like that of a mother on a journey with her child. Fearing that robbers may come to take the boy captive, she places him behind her. Aware that a wolf may attack from behind, she places him in front. If robbers come in front and wolves in the rear, she takes the child in her arms. If he is troubled by the heat, she covers him with her own garment. If he becomes hungry, she gives him food; thirsty, she gives him something to drink. Thus did God do for Israel while they wandered in the desert."

Mechilta, Beshallach 4

In an effort to summarize the core principles of Jewish belief, the great medieval philosopher and theologian Moses Maimonides prepared a series of thirteen creedal statements, aptly called the Thirteen Articles of Faith. You can find them in most prayer books (either in their original form or recast in the Yigdal hymn). Each of the statements begins with the words "I believe with complete faith," something many of us today find difficult to say.

While it would be nice to be as certain as Maimonides was about our religious beliefs, our hesitation stems from more than the objection that Judaism cannot be reduced to a series of brief statements. Nowadays we are just not comfortable with belief statements, and prefer to express our basic belief system through our prayers, often in metaphoric form.

Judaism demands more than the acceptance of a complex system of beliefs. Rather, Judaism insists on behavior that nourishes a relationship to the holy. Moreover, Jews do not generally feel comfortable about expressing their faith to others. Some think that it does not "feel Jewish" to do so. Others have not given any thought to their personal beliefs, simply coasting through Jewish life (or not), accepting what rabbis and other teachers tell them. They seldom think through the personal impact of statements of faith, instead allowing them to devolve into platitudes.

Faith begins in personal examination and then in dialogue. From an examination of your personal beliefs about God, you can come to understand exactly (or approximately) what you believe.

While an articulation of a personal conviction is a place to start, faith for Jews also comprises acceptance of the constant struggle that faith implies. We may wish it were more simple, but, like life, it just isn't. This may seem somewhat circular, but as we encounter the realities of the world each day, our faith in God forces us to grapple with what we believe.

To be sure, the complexity of the world and the familiarity of our lives provide us with a great deal to challenge our beliefs and our faith. We can either keep our religious beliefs separate from our encounters with the world or we can allow them to be the prism through which we view the world.

And so, throughout our history, individual Jews have assumed the posture of *chutzpah clappei malah* ("chutzpah in the face of heaven"), a way of challenging God, holding God responsible for what the world is and how it operates. We constantly challenge God, argue with God, confront God, level charges of injustice against God. But throughout this process, one thing remains clear: we are not denying God.

Of the great figures in the history of Judaism, Levi Yitzchak of Berditchev is probably the best known for assuming the posture of loving struggle with the Deity. There are many stories about his persistent bargaining with God on behalf of the Jewish people. Just as God requires us to maintain our part of the covenantal relationship, Levi Yitzchak demands that God be faithful to the divine end of the bargain made with the Israelites at Sinai. Elie Weisel, a survivor of the horror of the Holocaust, once remarked, "A Jew can be Jewish with God, against God, but not without God."

Ironically, this struggle is what confirms our belief, for our days are filled with simple miracles, too frequently overlooked, that help us to affirm our faith. Yet we often walk "sightless among them." The Baal Shem Tov taught it this way: "It is written, 'They are new every morning: great is your faith' (Lamentations 3:23). Believe that the world is created anew every day, and that you are reborn each morning. Your faith will then be increased and you will take a fresh interest in your daily service to Adonai."

It may surprise you to know that faith comes with difficulty, especially to the religious person. The religious life is never easy and not a simple pursuit. As we all eventually learn, nothing worthwhile is easy, and this is especially true for the religious life, since it opens the possibility of soaring heavenward while remaining firmly planted in the world. Regardless of the current state of our religious life, all of us have the potential to aspire to faith. If we want to believe, we must work toward belief.

Jewish thinkers have often not focused on the nature of faith, and as a result it is sometimes argued that theology is not a central concern of Judaism. And yet in our time we have passed through the most horrific period of Jewish existence, during which many Jews retained and even deepened their faith. Some even sang of the coming of the Messiah as they made their way into the gas chambers. There can be no more powerful statement of Jewish faith than to say that it is eternal and indestructible, even by supreme evil.

Faith embraces us when we are at peace, and sustains and protects us when we are most vulnerable. Without faith, we would be unable to stand; without faith, we would have no sense of being pulled upward toward something, always higher, always beyond our selves.

Knowing, Being, Doing
Reflect on a belief that you once held or were once taught. Think about it for a while. Say it aloud. Consider how it sounds when you hear it. Consider why you might have been taught that particular notion. Now ponder it in the face of the reality you have encountered as you have grown older. Has anything changed your perception of the subject of the belief?

Work the original statement of the belief into a statement that still holds power for you. Say it aloud and share it with someone else.

More on Expressing Disbelief/Embracing Faith

Woe to those who desecrate the name of heaven, for thus have our sages of blessed memory said, "If you are guilty of desecrating the Name, repentance alone will not suspend punishment, nor will atoning on Yom Kippur, nor will purging by afflictions, but all three are needed to suspend, and death consummates the atonement, as it written, 'And it was revealed in my ears by Adonai Tzeva'ot: Surely, this iniquity shall not be forgiven you until you die' (Isaiah 22:14)" (Babylonian Talmud, Yoma 86a). And our sages said further, "No allowance is given for the desecration of the Name, whether inadvertent or deliberate" (Babylonian Talmud, Kiddushin 40a). This means that if you sin in this way you are not dealt with like a shopkeeper giving credit; in other words, heaven does not wait to punish you but exacts retribution immediately. Or if you are half-innocent and half-guilty, and among your transgressions is that of desecration of the Name, it turns the balance and you emerge guilty.

Sefer Ma'alot Ha-Middot

When Rabbi Yitzchak of Getz was a little boy, his mother took him to see the Maggid of Koznitz. While they were waiting to see the Maggid, someone said to him, "I'll give you a coin if you can tell me where God lives." The boy thought for a moment and replied, "I'll give you a coin if you can tell me where God does not live."

Who can understand the mystery of Your acts?
For You have given our bodies the means to do Your work.
You gave us eyes to see Your signs,
Ears to hear Your wonders,
A mind to comprehend some part of Your secrets,
A mouth to speak Your praises,
A tongue to tell everyone Your mighty acts,
As, today, do I,
Your servant, the son of Your handmaid,
Who tells, according to the limit of my tongue,
A bit of a part of Your greatness.

Solomon ibn Gabirol
excerpted from The Kingly Crown

Where I wander—You!
Where I ponder—You!
Only You, You again, always You!
You! You! You!
When I am gladdened—You!
When I am saddened—You!
Only You, You again, always You!
You! You! You!
Sky is You, earth is You!
You above! You below!
In every trend, at every end,
Only You, You again, always You!
You! You! You!

Levi Yitzchak of Berditchev

I believe that what I believe is less important than what I do; yet I believe that much of what I do is the result of what I believe. I would want to say not so much, "I believe," as "I wish to believe" so to shape my life that it is a living testimony bespeaking what I believe.

Rabbi Zalman Schachter-Shalomi

Faith is not sweet, docile acceptance of God's mercy and compassion. Faith is dialogue with God, the process of getting our stubborn, sometimes stupid, wills to a unity of will. We have to keep trying even when we think God is silent, asking questions even at the risk of being disillusioned, crossing the frontier of noisy events that surge around us until we enter the stillness of the small voice.

Rabbi Arnold Kaiman

CHAPTER 22

Forgetting/Creating Memory

Shichechah/Zikaron

*We were slaves to Pharaoh in Egypt. But Adonai
brought us forth with a mighty hand and with an outstretched arm. If the Holy One had not taken our
ancestors out of Egypt, then we and our children and
our children's children would still be enslaved. . . . It is
our duty to tell the story of the Exodus.*

Passover Haggadah

*My father was a wandering Aramean and he went
down into Egypt and sojourned there. Few in number,
he became a great nation, great, mighty, and populous.
And the Egyptians dealt ill with us and afflicted us
and laid hard bondage upon us. So we cried to Adonai,
the God of our ancestors, and Adonai heard our voice,
saw our affliction, our toil and oppression. Then
Adonai brought us forth out of Egypt with a mighty
hand and an outstretched arm, with great, awesome
signs and wonders. And God brought us to this place
and gave us this land, a land flowing with milk and
honey.*

Deuteronomy 25:5–9

Remember that we were slaves. Remember the covenant that God made with us. Remember Shabbat. Remember to remember and not to forget. The Bible tells us our history, even how to remember it. Yet the most crucial aspect of remembering is less the reading of the history than the ritualized reenactment and retelling of it.

Remembering is our way of making community. Memory (*zikaron*) is our way of maintaining a relationship with God. Memory is our way of knowing who we are. We are a people obsessed with remembering. We name our children after our deceased parents and grandparents to keep their memory alive. We reiterate the names of our biblical ancestors—Abraham and Sarah, Isaac and Rebecca, Jacob, Leah, and Rachel—at every turn in our prayer book and our religious life. Rather than say their names only when they occur in the weekly readings of the Torah, we recall their names daily in prayer. We don't just remember them, we live with them.

The pedagogy of *zikaron* is intense and unrelenting: Remember in every possible way. Repeat the laws of Shabbat every Shabbat. Reaccept the Torah on Shavuot as our predecessors did at Mount Sinai. Reenact the joy of every holiday. Retell the story of the Exodus through the Haggadah every Passover. "We were slaves in

Egypt." On Sukkot, redo the booths our ancestors lived in when they were still agriculturalists.

"This is the time of our rejoicing." We drink and dance to remember redemption on Purim. "We praise God for the miracles done for our ancestors," rekindling the lights on Chanukah to remember the miracle of the oil and the Maccabees. All to remember miracles and to teach why we do what we do; how we have become who we are. There is a mantra of narratives. We memorize them, sing them, and internalize them. We remember them.

The verb *zachar* appears in various forms no less than 169 times in the Hebrew Bible. Usually it's God or Israel that is remembering (or failing to remember, as is often the case with Israel failing to remember God). In *Zachor*, a major work on Jewish history, Yosef Yerushalmi maintains that memory became crucial to the faith of the Jewish people and, ultimately, to their very existence. Without history, and without our remembering it, there is no peoplehood, no faith. Memory, says Yerushalmi, flows through two channels: ritual and recital. The Passover seder, lighting Chanukah candles— these are ritualized recitations of the stories which create memory.

Today, however, the majority of the Jewish people lives without much ritual and with even less recital of those crucial aspects of the Bible and our history that are essential for Jewish survival. It is as if there were a kind of subconscious memory, a latent memory that perseveres even when not conscious. The power of Jewish memory, even in the absence of Jewish knowledge or Jewish behavior, is apparent whenever Jews begin to identify themselves after generations of assimilation, hiding, and conversion. Certainly this is what has happened with many immigrants from the former Soviet Union. In their new homes in Israel or America, they dig out their lineage and their heirlooms, and begin to remember. Guided by members of the Jewish community, they celebrate holidays and life-cycle events, often for the first time in three generations. New Jewish memories are created where previously there were none.

An extreme case of the exertion of Jewish memory on behalf of one who did not remember was reported in the Jewish press a few years ago: the corpses of Jewish men who had immigrated to Israel from the former Soviet Union were being circumcised before burial. The mark that distinguishes the flesh of Jewish males, initiated by Abraham to recall the covenant he had made with God for himself and his descendants, was made upon these dead men. Their corpses were forced to remember what their bodies did not experience in life.

Many of us, immigrants and natives of countries with thriving Jewish communities alike, find ourselves in the position of creating Jewish memories. Often it is not simply a matter of beginning to recite texts or engage in rituals with some frequency. Creating a Jewish memory first means acknowledging a Jewish self and then gaining access to the books, materials, and skills necessary to engage in the recitation and ritual action that is at the core of Jewish memory. Kerry's family collects Noah's arks so whenever the family travels, his son Jesse goes on the prowl, looking for a new one to add to the collection. He does the same thing with draydels and kiddush cups and *hanukiyot*, whatever breathes new life into Jewish ritual.

Hundreds and thousands of Jews in America and throughout the world are learning the Alephbet even as you read these lines. Thousands are experiencing Shabbat for the first time. And many are beginning to celebrate Jewish holidays and lifecycle events with the intention of creating Jewish memories for their children—memories that they themselves do not have.

Sometimes remembering is also about forgetting. Years before her death, Kerry once asked his bubbe, the last of the Russian generation of his family, to tell him a little about her childhood in Russia. "Perhaps it was shtetl nostalgia or an acknowledgment of the command to remember. Looking me straight in the eye—the truth is she was barely four and a half feet tall—she said, 'Russia was terrible when I was a child. That is why we left and came to America. I have forgotten about it. Now you must forget about it too.' I often remember her story, thereby remembering to forget."

Much of the Jewish community's effort to create Jewish memories for those who do not have them is accompanied by an intense, usually unspoken belief: Memory saves. If we can begin by remembering what happened to us, we will remember who we are and what we are; and then we will have the possibility of survival and salvation.

Knowing, Being, Doing

Create a Jewish memory for yourself. Pick a day on the calendar that you do not currently observe or celebrate—Jerusalem Day (in the spring on the 29th of Iyar), perhaps, or the Fast of Gedaliah (in the fall on the 3rd of Tishrei). Mark the day with a ritual. Learn something new about it. Observe it in some way. Record for yourself what it was like, what you did not like. Next year, on the same day, read what you wrote the year before, and record your memory of it, and how it feels to have added that day to your Jewish calendar. Now you have created a Jewish memory.

More on Forgetting/Creating Memory

In the time of Mattitiyahu son of Jonathan, when the Greek rulers tried to make the Jews forget Your Torah . . . You were present for them and enabled them to find courage.

From the Amidah for Chanukah

Remember what Amalek did to you on the way as you came forth out of Egypt, how he met you on the way, and smote the rear of your caravan, all who were weak, when you were faint and weary, and he did not fear God. Therefore, it shall be when Adonai your God has granted you rest from all your enemies who surround you, in the land which Adonai your God gave you as an inheritance to possess it, that you shall blot out the remembrance of Amalek from under heaven; you shall not forget!

Deuteronomy 25:17–19

Rabbi Abbahu said, "For forty days Moses learned the details of the Torah, and he forgot them as quickly as he learned them. On the fortieth day the Torah was given to him as a gift, and he had no further difficulty in remembering it. By the same token, if you study diligently, do not despair because you forget what you have learned. In the proper time all of it will be firmly implanted in your memory."

Jerusalem Talmud, Horaiyot 3

There are stars up above
So far away we only see their light
Long long after the star itself is gone
And so it is with people that we loved
Their memories keep shining,
Ever brightly, though their time with us is done.
But the stars that light up the darkest night
These are the lights that guide us
As we live our days these are the ways
we remember, we remember.

Hebrew by Hannah Senesh
English translation by Cantor Jeff Klepper

In Judaism remembrance is not mere recollection, not only a mental exercise of an evanescent nature. Nor is it an emotional experience of the hurried moment, fleeting glimpses into the yesteryear. For us memory is the constant generator of history, human and divine.

Rabbi Nahum Schulman

CHAPTER 23

Seduced by Secularism/
Striving Toward Holiness
Chiloniut/Kedushah

*He who seeks an answer to the most pressing question,
what is living? will find an answer in the Bible: Man's
destiny is to be a partner rather than a master. There is
a task, a law, and a way: the task is redemption, the
law to do justice, to love mercy, and the way is the
secret of being human and holy. When we are gasping
with despair; when the wisdom of science and the
splendor of the arts fail to save us from fear and the
sense of futility, the Bible offers us the only hope: history is a circuitous way for the steps of the Messiah.*

Rabbi Abraham Joshua Heschel
God in Search of Man: A Philosophy of Judaism

Although we like to think we are in total control of our lives, much in our lives is beyond our control. Nonetheless, we are presented with endless choices, ways in which we can positively influence the world. While many of these choices may seem complicated, most of the time it is possible to distinguish between the two aspects of the world which compete to control us: those which are sacred and those which are not.

Rabbi Lawrence Kushner teaches that there is a purposeful difference between the sacred and the secular. Just as a Kiddush cup (used only for sacred purposes) differs from a paper cup (quickly used and then discarded), he argues, there is a vast difference between Jerusalem (which is potentially holy) and Las Vegas (which is wholly secular).

These contrasts exemplify the difference between the sacred and the profane, between what is holy and what is not holy (the "everyday," routine, or secular). The sacred and profane aspects of life constantly present themselves to us. It is up to us to choose between them. Or as Abraham Joshua Heschel said in *Man's Quest for God*: "The world is not a vacuum. Either we make it an altar for God or it is invaded by demons. There can be no neutrality. Either we are ministers of the sacred or slaves of evil."

At the end of the Torah, just before Moses dies and the Israelites enter the Promised Land, God stresses the importance of such choices: "See, I have set before you this day life and good, death and evil; in that I command you this day to love Adonai your God and to walk in God's ways. . . . I have set before you life and death, blessing and curse; therefore, choose life that you and your descendants may live" (Deuteronomy 30:15, 19).

God gives us the choice, even points out the downside of choosing what will lead us into world of curses; nevertheless, the decision is ours to make. This section of the Bible emphasizes, however, that loving God, living life according to God's laws, and doing *mitzvot* (fulfilling God's instructions) is tantamount to choosing life. In other words, when we join with God through Torah, we achieve life.

While choosing life is analogous to choosing blessing over curse in this passage, one must also actively choose holiness over the profane. One must seek ways to turn the secular, the baseness of everyday life, into something sacred. Heschel argues that one does not reach the sacred without moving first through the secular. He writes in *Man Is Not Alone* that "The road to the sacred leads through the secular."

Even the mystics suggest that the only way to reach the heavenly Jerusalem is through the earthly Jerusalem. Only by being present in the reality of the moment, however simple and common it may be, is there a possibility of making it sacred. Kerry first went to Israel at the age of sixteen. He recalls: "While my ancestors may have traveled by boat or caravan or even on foot, I traveled on the 'wings of eagles,' that is, on a jet airplane. I felt a little odd—but I kissed the tarmac nevertheless. I knew that there was something holy about that place—even though it looked just like lots of other airports in smaller cities around the United States."

In another passage, we are told to be a holy people because we belong to God, who is also holy (that is, wholly separate): "And you shall be holy to me, for I Adonai am holy" (Leviticus 20:26). We strive to achieve holiness by working and walking with God.

The Jewish people are often described as holy. Yet we are also associated with the strong human tendency to be less than holy; the

God of the Bible is constantly negotiating with us, pushing us to adopt higher standards of holiness and morality, yet fully accepting us where we are—so long as we are willing to reach higher.

People, things, times, and places can literally be "lifted up" out of their non-holy status into a state of being recognized as holy or sacred. Interestingly, we human beings usually do the lifting up. It is people who choose to engender holiness, even while it is God who teaches us the meaning and essence of holiness.

Knowing who and whose we are—that we are a holy people and that we belong to God, who is likewise holy—enables us to engage in acts of lifting up, of striving; of turning a moment, a place, a thing, into something greater than it once was thought to be.

We can do this with ourselves too. Note that "You shall be holy" is a stated direction toward the future; we are always in the process of becoming holy, of becoming more than we are, of becoming all that we can be. This does not mean becoming perfect. It means becoming more God-like than we currently are. As Menachem Mendl, the famed rabbi of Kotzk, explained, "You shall be holy unto Me" means, "As human beings; you shall be humanly unto Me."

The sages of the Mishnah and Talmud expanded the biblical view of holiness, raising it to an actual state of being: a status that a person or an object can attain. This state or status may even be inherent in an object or thing. Like a vessel used by the priests in the ancient Temple, holiness must be actively maintained and protected.

Objects are holy when they are used in conjunction with an activity or ritual that is holy. Common material is transformed into the sacred when it is separated from other kinds of material and used solely for a sacred purpose; that is the real difference between the Kiddush cup and the paper cup. In fact, using a paper cup for Kiddush can make it holy—if only for the moment.

There is no guarantee that an object will remain holy after reaching this state. When Kerry's son, Avi, was young, he would play in the kitchen while the family prepared for Shabbat dinner on Friday evening. Once he took the challah from the table when his parents weren't looking, went into a corner of the room, and began nibbling its ends. Although no longer a perfect twist, somehow that was the sweetest challah the Olitzkys had ever tasted!

According to the sages, people can also become holy vessels. When you make yourself into a conduit for what is most important—making yourself of use to the community by performing some sacred act—you become a holy vessel. In traditional usage, the term *klei kodesh* is applied to those who lead the community in prayer, as it was to those who performed the priestly functions in the ancient Temple and approached the Holy of Holies, its innermost sanctum, on Yom Kippur.

Even without any kind of public role, we can all transform ourselves into holy vessels. We can set aside certain objects for a sacred purpose or celebrate the holy days on our calendar. We can seek out the sacred places in our lives and make them holy or simply act as a channel through which God's work is done in the world, especially in our relationships with others.

Here, Rabbi Heschel is instructive once again. "Judaism is a theology of the common deed . . . dealing not so much with the training for the exceptional, as with the management of the trivial. The predominant feature in the Jewish pattern of life is unassuming, inconspicuous piety rather than extravagance, mortification, asceticism. Thus, the purpose seems to be to ennoble the common, to endow worldly things with higher beauty; to attune the comparative to the absolute, to associate the detail with the whole, to adapt our own being with its plurality, conflicts, and contradictions, to the all-transcending unity, to the holy."

Knowing, Being, Doing

Begin to recognize the *klei kodesh*—objects brimming with the potential to achieve holiness—in your home.

Make an accounting of the ways in which you act as a holy vessel, serving as an instrument for God's work in the world. Here's a list to get you started: love-making with your spouse, parenthood, teaching, healing, defending justice, feeding the hungry, protecting the vulnerable.

More on Seduced by Secularism/Striving Toward Holiness

Knowledge of the Torah leads to watchfulness, watchfulness to zeal, zeal to cleanliness, cleanliness to abstinence, abstinence to purity, purity to saintliness, saintliness to humility, humility to the fear of sin, and the fear of sin to holiness.

Babylonian Talmud, Avodah Zarah 20b

Rabbi Nachman of Bratzlav taught that Israel's holiness is entirely dependent on the Land of Israel. Whenever an individual Jew undergoes purification and sanctification, a piece of the land is conquered and redeemed.

Life passes on in proximity to the sacred, and it is this proximity that endows existence with ultimate significance. In our relation to the immediate we touch upon the most distant. Even the satisfaction of physical needs can be a sacred act. Perhaps the essential message of Judaism is that in doing the finite we may perceive the infinite.

Abraham Joshua Heschel

Rabbi David Moshe of Tchortkov, who was not very big or strong, once had to hold a Torah scroll for a long time while it was being consecrated. After a while, one of the men in the community, who was much bigger than Rabbi David Moshe, asked whether the rabbi wanted him to take it for a while. Rabbi David Moshe responded, "The ark of the covenant that our ancestors carried in the desert was very heavy. It was nearly impossible to lift. But once it was lifted, it actually carried the men who lifted it. Once you hold something holy, it isn't heavy anymore."

In teaching his grandson Avi, Abe Olitzky (Kerry's father) added to what Rabbi David Moshe said: "As long as you carry the words of the Torah in your heart, they will carry you."

Rabbi Abraham Isaac Kook taught that we begin to absorb traces of holiness little by little. One point of light after another flashes on us, like falling drops of rain. These heaven-sent elements, as they gather together within us, become a great flaming torch. They concentrate their foundation within our souls, and the paths they carve pierce through to the essence of our being.

Do not turn your heart away from meditating upon the words of Torah and holiness, lest your heart be empty and void of reflection on the commandments, and in order that your heart may become a dwelling place for the Shechinah.

Moses Cordovero
Tomer Devorah

Glossary of Terms and Concepts

Aleph-bet. The Hebrew alphabet

Acheiruta. Otherness, differentness.

Ahavah. Love.

Aleynu. Concluding prayer of daily service, declaring messianic hope that all will one day worship one God; originated in High Holy Day liturgy.

Amidah. Lit. "standing." Core section of daily liturgy, said while standing, hence name. Also called *Shemoneh Esreh* ("eighteen"), because it originally was made up of eighteen blessings (a nineteenth was later added), and *Ha-Tefillah* ("the prayer"), a name indicating its importance as the prayer par excellence.

Anavah. Humility.

Anochiut. Self-centeredness, self-oriented behavior.

Apikorsus. Disbelief in some element of Jewish tradition or Torah and rabbinic law.

Am ha-artzut. Person ignorant of Jewish teachings or Jewish law.

Aritzut. Abuse of power.

Avodah. Lit. "work." Sacred or holy work; ritual service in ancient Temple; prayer.

Ayin. Nothingness.

B'gidah. Betrayal, deception.

B'tzelem elohim. Lit. "in the image of God." From Genesis 1:27, describing how humans were created.

Boorut. Ignorance.

Brit. Covenant, agreement.

Chesed. Righteous, kind, unusual.

Cheshbon hanefesh. Lit. "accounting of the soul." Introspection, self-examination.

Chevruta. Study partner; method of learning with another person.

Chiloniut. Secularity, secularism.

Chochmah. Wisdom, knowledge.

De'agah. Worry, concern, anxiety.

Devekut. Lit. "cleaving." Mystical goal of cleaving to God during prayer.

Dibbuk chaverim. Cleaving faithfully to a friend; commitment between two people.

Dika'on. Depression, lowliness.

Emunah. Faith.

Gemilut chasadim. Righteous acts of giving with generosity, both of time and of other resources.

Hallel. Group of psalms recited on festivals and first days of each month.

Hashlayah. Self-deprecation; deceiving oneself.

Hashkiveinu. Prayer recited in evening requesting that God protect Israel.

He-azat Panim. Haughty arrogance.

Hefkerut. Living blasphemously.

Hoda'ah. Thankfulness, thanksgiving.

Kabbalah. Jewish mystical teachings.

Kamtzanut. Stinginess, selfishness.

Kedushah. Holiness, that which is sacred.

Kefiut tovah. Lit. "insincere gratitude." Forcing a thank you.

Ketubah. Marriage document, given by husband to wife, validated by signatures of two witnesses.

Lashon hara. Lit. "evil tongue." Gossip, rumormongering.

Lashon hatov. Lit. "good tongue." Language which increases positive feelings and perceptions of others.

Madreigot. Stairs, stairway, steps.

Mechilah. Forgiveness, pardon for sin or transgression against God or another person.

Mensch. One who has the traits of a human being—generosity, sensitivity, kindness, decency, etc.

Menschlichkeit. Lit. "being a human being." The quality of acting like a mensch.

Middot. Moral guidance or attributes.

Mitzvah. Commandment to do a particular act, usually based on Torah; divine instruction.

Musar. Jewish moral teachings.

Pikuach nefesh. Commandment to save and protect human life.

Rachmanut. Compassion, expressing compassion.

Remiach. Deception, betrayal.

Rosh Hashanah. Jewish New Year.

Sasson. Happiness, joy.

Sefer. Book; most often a book of Torah learning.

Shalem. Whole, complete.

Shalvah. Tranquility

Shechinah. God's feminine aspect; the Divine Presence.

Shelemut. Completion, wholeness, integrity.

Shichechah. Forgetting, forgetfulness

Simchah. Happiness, joy.

Sinah. Hatred.

Tallit. Prayer shawl, fringed garment worn during morning prayers and by prayer leader; often used as bridal canopy.

Tefillah. Lit. "prayer." With definite article used as alternative designation for Amidah.

Teshuvah. Repentance, return, renewal.

Tikkun olam. Repair or renovation of world; sometimes shortened to *tikkun*, repair.

Tikvah. Hope, hopefulness.

Tzaddik-in-peltz. Lit. "a righteous person in a fur coat." Yiddish expression.

Tzedakah. Sacred giving, charity, justice, giving righteously.

Tzimtzum. Contraction of self; usually, God's contraction in order to allow room for world to be created.

Tzeniut. Modest dress and behavior, protecting human body from humiliation or unnecessary exposure.

Unataneh tokef. Liturgical piece recited on Yom Kippur.

Yeridah. Descent, moving downward.

Yetzer hara. Lit. "evil inclination." Acts based on self-interest, natural bodily urges.

Yetzer tov. Lit. "good inclination." Inclination to act ethically and according to God's laws.

Ye'ush. Despair.

Yom Kippur. Day of Atonement.

Zenut. Promiscuous sexual behavior; prostitution, exploiting the body.

Zikaron. Memory, remembering.

Our Rabbis and Teachers

Abbaye bar Chalil (ca. 280–338): Known for his noble character and keenness of mind; chosen to lead talmudic academy in Pumbedita as result of his resolution of a technical legal problem.

Akiva (ca. 50–135): Famous Palestinian sage of Mishnah, known for influence on development of Jewish law. Became scholar late in life and had many students. Was leader of rabbinic academy and politically active in supporting Bar Kokhba revolt.

Joseph Albo (15th cent.): Philosopher, theologian, student of Chasdai Crescas, best known for *Sefer Ha-Ikkarim* and its discussion of dogmas in Judaism.

Baruch of Midzbizh (1757–1810): Grandson of Baal Shem Tov, Chasidic master, and author of *Butzina Kaddisha*.

Hillel Bavli (1893-1961): Born in Lithuania, migrated to United States in 1912. Hebrew poet and professor of Hebrew literature at Jewish Theological Seminary. Translated works of Shakespeare and Dickens into Hebrew.

Jules Harlow (1931–   ): Rabbi, liturgist; edited daily, Sabbath, and High Holy Day prayer books for Conservative movement.

Abraham Joshua Heschel (1907–1972): Born near Warsaw of Chasidic lineage, educated in Vilna and Berlin. Brought to United States in 1940 by Hebrew Union College, where he taught until 1945. Later, professor of philosophy and theology at Jewish Theological Seminary. Best known for his theological writings, including *Man Is Not Alone* and *God in Search of Man*. Active in civil rights movement in early 1960s.

Hillel (1st cent. B.C.E.): Born in Babylonia and settled in Palestine. Appointed president of Sanhedrin. Together with Shammai, was last of "pairs" of scholars known as *zugot*.

Rabbi Judah (ca. 135–220): Patriarch of Palestinian Jewry, compiler/editor of Mishnah. Known during his lifetime as Rabbenu Ha-Kadosh and usually referred to in Talmud simply as "Rabbi."

Abraham J. Karp (1921–   ): Conservative rabbi and American Jewish historian who served Beth El of Rochester, New York, 1956–1972.

Abraham Isaac HaKohen Kook (1865–1935): Of Chasidic descent and educated at Volozhin yeshiva in Lithuania; emigrated to Palestine at turn of century; became chief rabbi of Jaffa and later first Ashkenazi chief rabbi of Palestine. His writings, infused with mystical teachings, stressed centrality of Jewish nationalism and Land of Israel. Created environment which allowed for inclusion and tolerance among religious and nonreligious settlers. Well known for *Orot Ha-Teshuvah*, on repentance, and his collected teachings published posthumously, *Orot Ha-Kodesh*.

Levi bar Sissi (3rd cent.): Born in Palestine, usually referred to in Talmud without title Rabbi, although he was a sage and one of Rabbi Judah's last disciples.

Levi Yitzchak of Berditchev (1740–1809): Student of Dov Baer of Mezritch and leading figure of Chasidism in Poland and Ukraine. Authored prayers and supplications in Yiddish. Teachings collected in *Kiddushat Levi*.

Moses Chaim Luzzatto (1707–1747): Kabbalist and poet also known as Ramchal, head of center of Jewish learning in Padua, Italy. Had strong messianic aspirations and was exiled to Amsterdam. Many of his books were burned by opponents. Works include *Mesillat Yesharim*, ethical treatise, and *Derech Ha-Shem*, popular kabbalistic work.

Moses Maimonides (1135–1204): Famous philosopher, legal codifier, and medical writer. Born in Cordova, Spain; left at early age to escape Almamohade persecutions. In youth, wrote commentary to entire Mishnah in Arabic and, in 1180, completed monumental codification of Jewish law, *Mishneh Torah*. In 1190, completed *Guide of Perplexed*, single most important statement of medieval Jewish philosophy.

Jacob Rader Marcus (1896–1995): Reform rabbi who shaped field of American Jewish history, teaching at Hebrew Union College in Cincinnati for over 70 years. Established American Jewish Archives in 1947.

Nachman of Bratzlav (1772–1810): Great-grandson of Baal Shem Tov. One of most influential Chasidic masters of 18th cent., taught simple faith emphasizing importance of prayer and music. Teachings collected in *Likkutei Moharan* and *Sipurei Ma'asiot*.

Philo of Alexandria (ca. 20 B.C.E.–40 C.E.): Hellenistic Jewish philosopher known for allegorical approach to Bible commentary and philosophical interpretation of Scripture.

Ellis Rivkin (1918–   ): Innovative Jewish historian who applied principles of economic determinism to development of leadership models in Jewish history and other problems of Jewish historiography.

Franz Rosenzweig (1886–1929): German philosopher who rediscovered Judaism on Yom Kippur in 1913. Author of *The Star of Redemption*, monumental work of Jewish philosophy, written primarily while serving in German army in World War I. Collaborated with Martin Buber to compose first major German translation of Scripture since Martin Luther.

Israel Salanter (1810–1883): Born in Lithuania, leader of Musar movement in Germany and Eastern Europe. Some of his writings collected in *Or Yisrael*.

Simcha Bunem of Przysucha (1767–1827): Polish Chasidic rebbe; disciple of Rabbi Jacob Isaac Horowitz (Seer of Lublin) and Rabbi Jacob Isaac Rabinowitz of Przysucha ("Holy Yehudi"). His teaching diminished emphasis on role of Tzaddik and raised value of conventional Torah study. Became leader of Chasidic sect and had profound impact on development of Chasidism in 19th-cent. Poland. Teachings found in *Kol Simcha, Midrash Simcha, Kol Mevasser,* and *Siach Sarfei Kodesh*.

Shimon ben Azzai (early 2nd cent.): According to tradition, one of four scholars who engaged in mystical practices; as a result died prematurely (see Chaggigah 14b for complete story). May have been one of ten sages martyred in Hadrianic persecutions which culminated in Bar Kokhba revolt.

Danny Siegel (1944–   ): Author, poet, lecturer, known for efforts to collect and distribute tzedakah, popularize acts of tzedakah, and spread stories of tzedakah heros. Also known for modern interpretations of midrash, books for children, and works teaching tzedakah, including *Gym Shoes and Irises*, *Where Heaven and Earth Touch*, and *Teach Me a Mitzvah*.

Nathan Sternhartz of Nemerov (1780–1844): Leading disciple of Rabbi Nachman of Bratzlav, editor of Nachman's collected teachings, *Likkutei Moharan*. Laid foundations for Bratzlaver Chasidism. Author of many works including multivolume commentary on *Shulchan Aruch* based on teachings of Rabbi Nachman.

Our Sacred Texts

Avot d'Rabbi Natan: Small tractate usually printed in Babylonian Talmud as commentary to *Pirke Avot*.

Ben Sirach, Wisdom of: Included in Apocrypha; lays down moral precepts against extremism and advocates moderation. Author was learned sage living in Jerusalem (2nd cent. B.C.E.).

Genesis Rabbah: Midrashic commentary on Book of Genesis.

Derech Eliyahu Zuta: Collection of moral discourses by Abba Elijah (10th cent.), focusing on love of Torah, humankind, Israel, and God.

Emet Kenah: Work of unknown origin; probably Chasidic text dating to 19th cent.

Exodus Rabbah: Midrashic commentary on Book of Exodus.

Hilchot Teshuvah: Section of *Mishneh Torah* of Maimonides dealing with repentance, especially focusing on laws of months of Elul and Tishrei.

Jeremiah: Biblical book containing prophecies of Jeremiah (7th–6th cent. B.C.E.), who rebuked Israelites for idolatry and immoral behavior, foretold destruction of First Temple, and is traditionally regarded as author of Book of Lamentations.

Kohelet: Known as Ecclesiastes in English; one of five scrolls in *Ketuvim* (Writings) section of Bible. Traditionally ascribed to Solomon, *Kohelet* is read in synagogue on Sukkot.

Kohelet Rabbah: Midrash on Book of Ecclesiastes.

Kotzker Ma'asiot: Collection of stories attributed to Menachem Mendl of Kotzk, the Kotzker Rebbe.

Leviticus Rabbah: Midrashic commentary on Book of Leviticus.

Likkutei Etzot Ha-Shalem: Book of advice organized according to moral attributes; attributed to Rabbi Nachman of Bratzlav; written by Nathan Sternhartz of Nemerov, his chief disciple.

Likkutei Tefillot: Book of prayers based on teachings of Rabbi Nachman of Bratzlav; by Nathan Sternhartz of Nemerov.

Menorat Ha-Ma'or: Collection of sermons and aggadic teachings emphasizing ethics of Judaism; by Yitzchak Aboab (14th cent.).

Mishneh Torah: First comprehensive codification of Jewish law; by Moses Maimonides (12th cent.).

Numbers Rabbah: Midrashic collection on Book of Numbers. Sections 15–23 are essentially *Midrash Tanchuma*.

Orchot Tzaddikim: Collection of medieval ethical texts by unknown author, first published in Prague.

Pesikta Rabbati: Collection of midrashic texts comprising 48 homilies on holidays and special Sabbaths of year, probably compiled in Palestine.

Pirke Avot: Tractate of Mishnah usually called *Ethics of the Fathers*. Traditionally studied on Sabbath afternoons from Passover until High Holidays, often incorporated into Sabbath prayer book. Last chapter, called *Kinyan Torah* or *Perek Rebbe Meir*, focuses on value of Torah study.

Reishit Chochma: Kabbalistic ethical treatise by Elijah da Vidas (16th cent.), focusing on ascetic and devotional practices in mystical context.

Ruth Rabbah: Midrashic commentary on Book of Ruth.

Seder Eliyahu Rabbah: Aggadic midrash on Book of Genesis, utilizing texts from Prophets and Book of Psalms.

Sefer Ma'alot Ha-Middot: Work by Rabbi Yechiel ben Yekutiel ben Benjamin Ha-Rofe of Rome (13th cent.) blending biblical and rabbinic statements as insights into moral living, categorizing them into series of virtues and vices.

Tanna d'Bei Eliyahu: Midrashic collection also known as *Seder Eliyahu*; unlike most collections of midrash, is uniform work utilizing original expressions.

Tanchuma: Midrashic collection compiled by Solomon Buber in 1885, reflects unique combination of halakhic and aggadic material attributed to Rabbi Tanchuma.

Teshuvot ha-Rashbah: Compilation of halakhic decisions on legal issues raised in Spain, the responsa of Rabbi Solomon ben Abraham Ibn Adret (ca. 1235–1310).

Tosefta: Supplement to Mishnah attributed to Nehemiah, disciple of Rabbi Akiva (Sanhedrin 86a). Contains alternative versions of mishnaic statements and sometimes includes statements and discussions not found in Mishnah.

Zohar: Most influential kabbalistic text of Middle Ages, first published in 1295 in Guadalajara, Spain, by Moses de Leon. Compilation of mystical interpretations of Shimon Bar Yochai, delivered during Hadrianic persecutions in 2nd cent.